Italianate Architecture in Ontario in Colour Photos, Saving Our History One Photo at a Time

Photography
by Barbara Raué
©2020

Series Name: Architectural Styles

Book 3: Italianate

Cover photo: 110 Ontario Street, Cobourg Book 3

©All the photos in this book have been taken with my cameras. I own the rights to them.

Italianate, 1850-1900 – A two story rectangular building with a mild hip roof, a projecting frontispiece, and generous eaves with ornate cornice brackets was the basis of the style; often there are large sash windows, quoins, ornate detailing on the windows, belvederes and wraparound verandahs. Italianate commercial buildings often have cast iron cresting and elegant window surrounds.

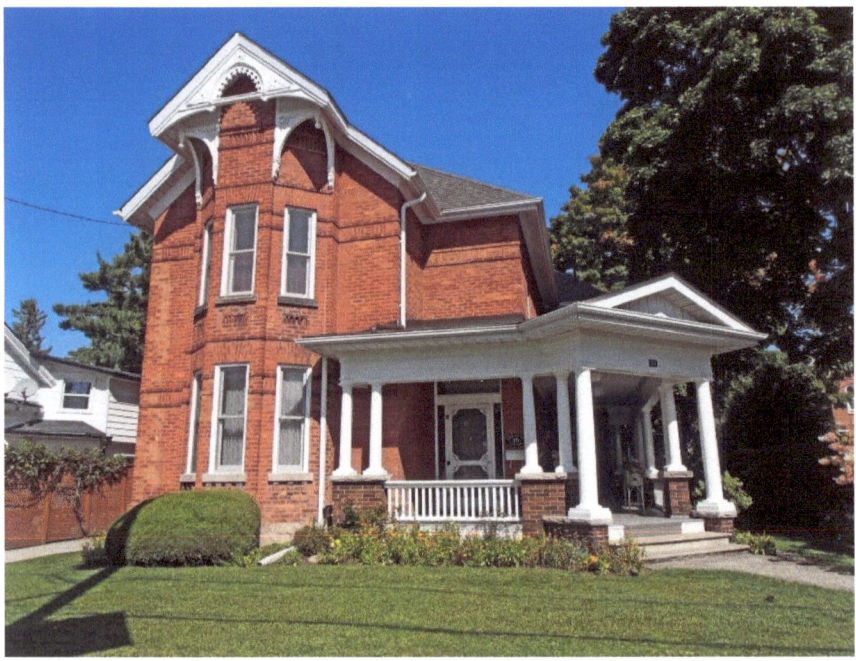

Acton - 39 Willow Street – Knox Manse established 1889 – Italianate with two-and-a-half storey tower-like bay, pediment above pillared porch, fretwork and verge board on gable

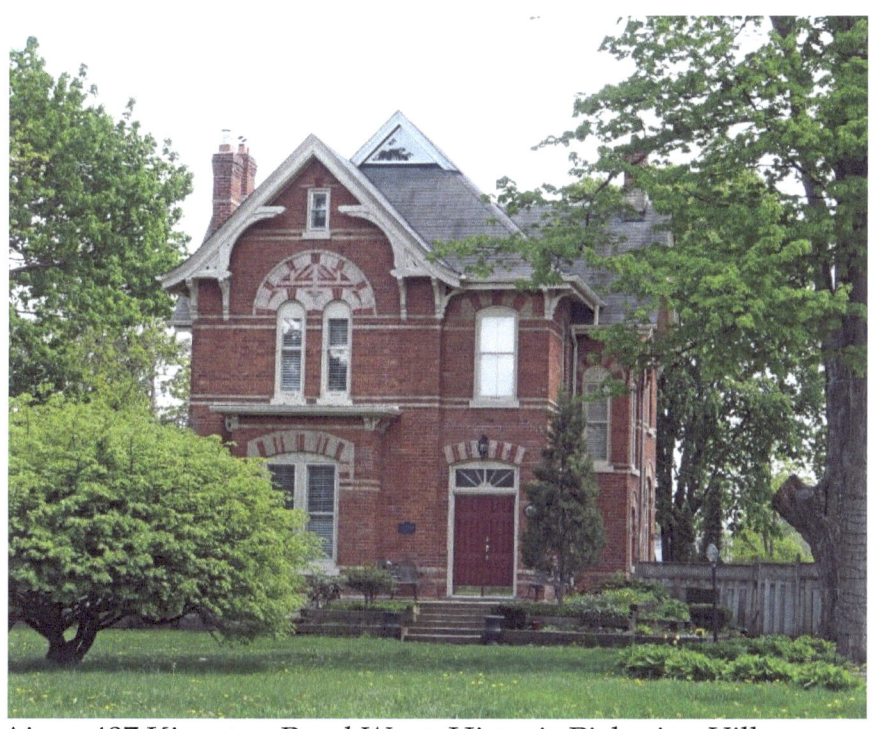

Ajax - 497 Kingston Road West, Historic Pickering Village – 1870 - purchased in 1882 by Dr. Field for his daughter. Dr. Field was a practicing physician in Pickering Village and later built his own home directly east of this property. In 1929, Emerson & Henrietta Bertrand purchased the home and raised Allan Irwin. The family gave up the homestead in 1934, only to have it reclaimed in 1977 by their grandson, B. B. Bertrand (son of Allan). The building is a 2½ storey brick structure in Italianate architecture.

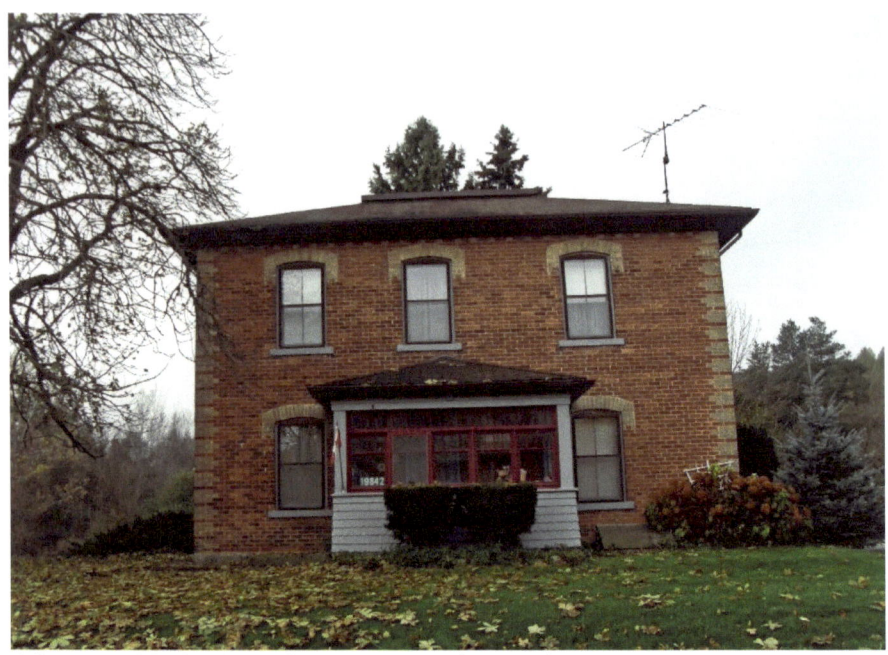

Alton - 19842 Main Street - Amelia and Peter V. Lemon House - circa 1886 - This two-storey Italianate style, red brick house with yellow brick detail has ten rooms, an enclosed front porch and a truncated hip roof. Local farmer Peter Lemon and his wife Amelia bought the house in 1887. Amelia was Nancy and Nicholas Smith's daughter. After her death, Peter sold the property to Alexander Menzies in 1896.

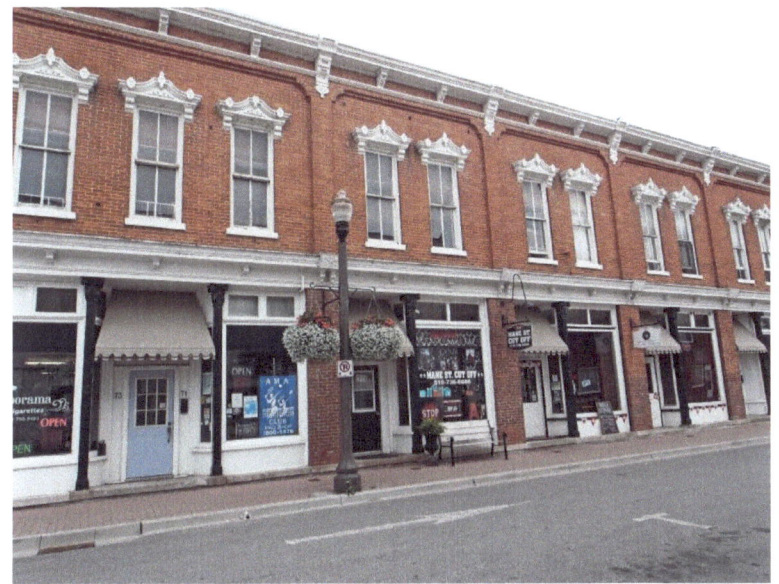

Amherstburg - 63-73 Murray Street – window hoods, cornice brackets, pilasters – Italianate commercial block - 1875

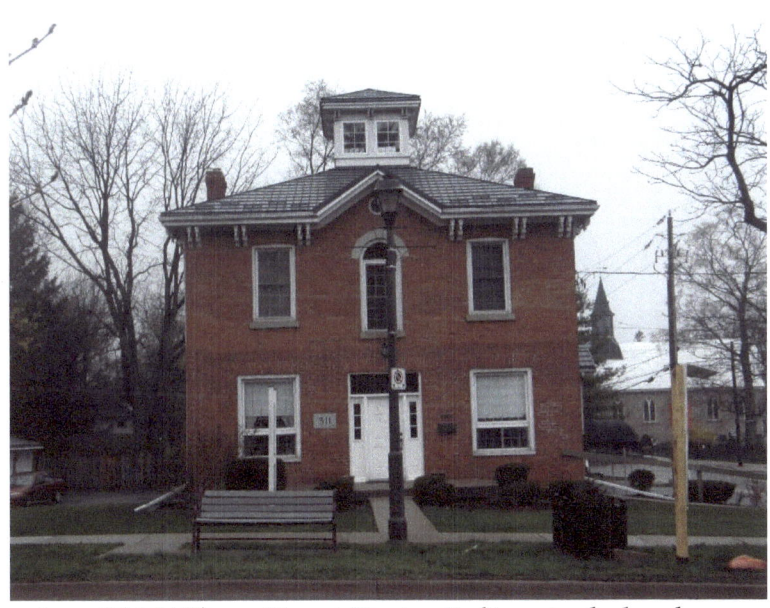

Ancaster - 311 Wilson Street East – Italianate, belvedere, paired cornice brackets

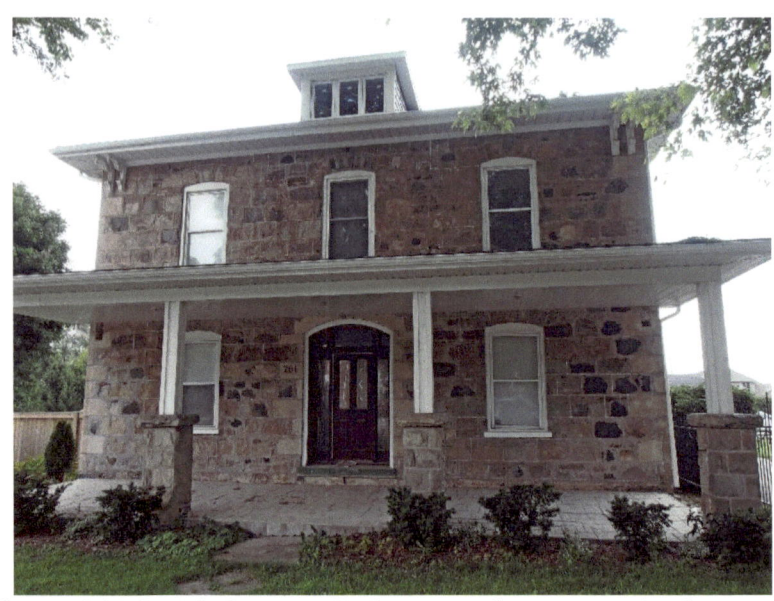

Arthur - 261 Smith Street – Italianate, dormer, paired cornice brackets, cobblestone architecture

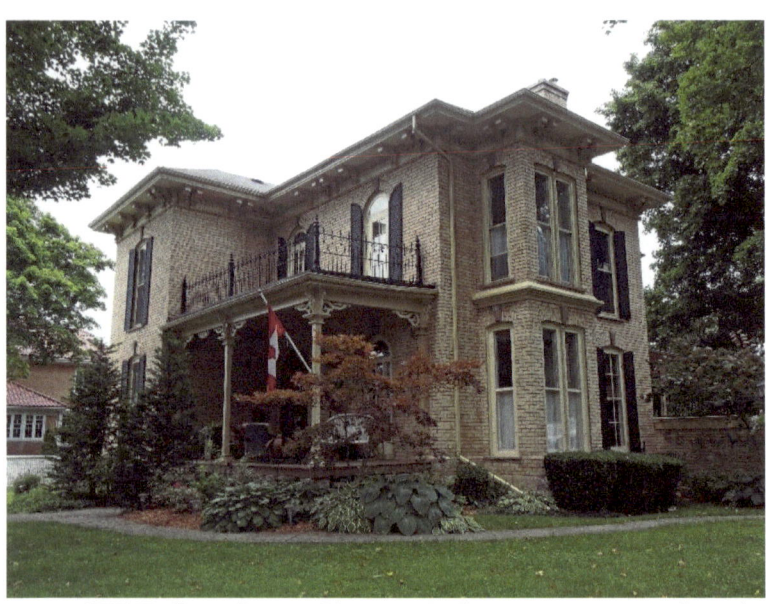

Aylmer - 375 Talbot Street West – Italianate, cornice brackets, two-storey tower-like bays, balcony on second floor

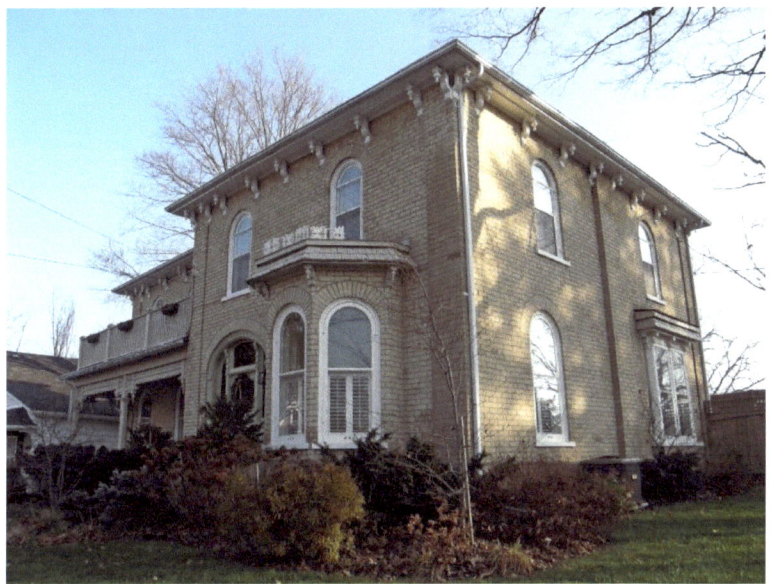

Ayr - Italianate - single cornice brackets, iron cresting above bay window

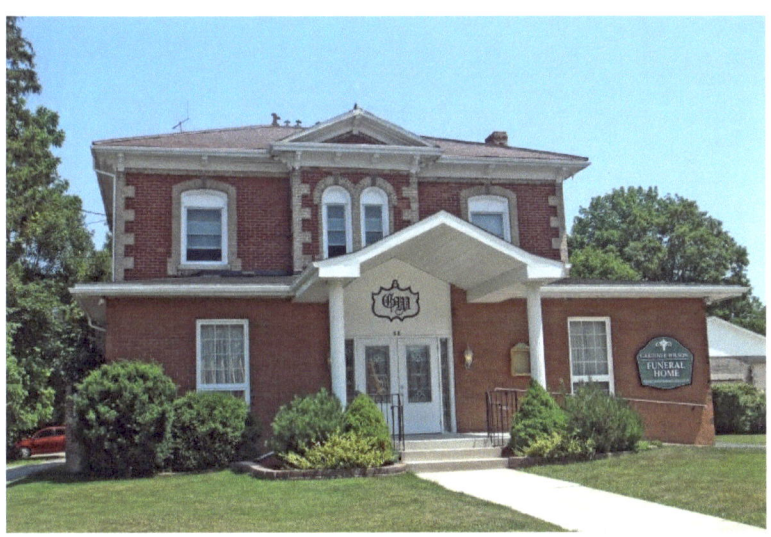

Beaver Valley Book – Meaford - 69 Denmark Street - Gardiner-Wilson Funeral Home – frontispiece topped with pediment, corner quoins, hipped roof

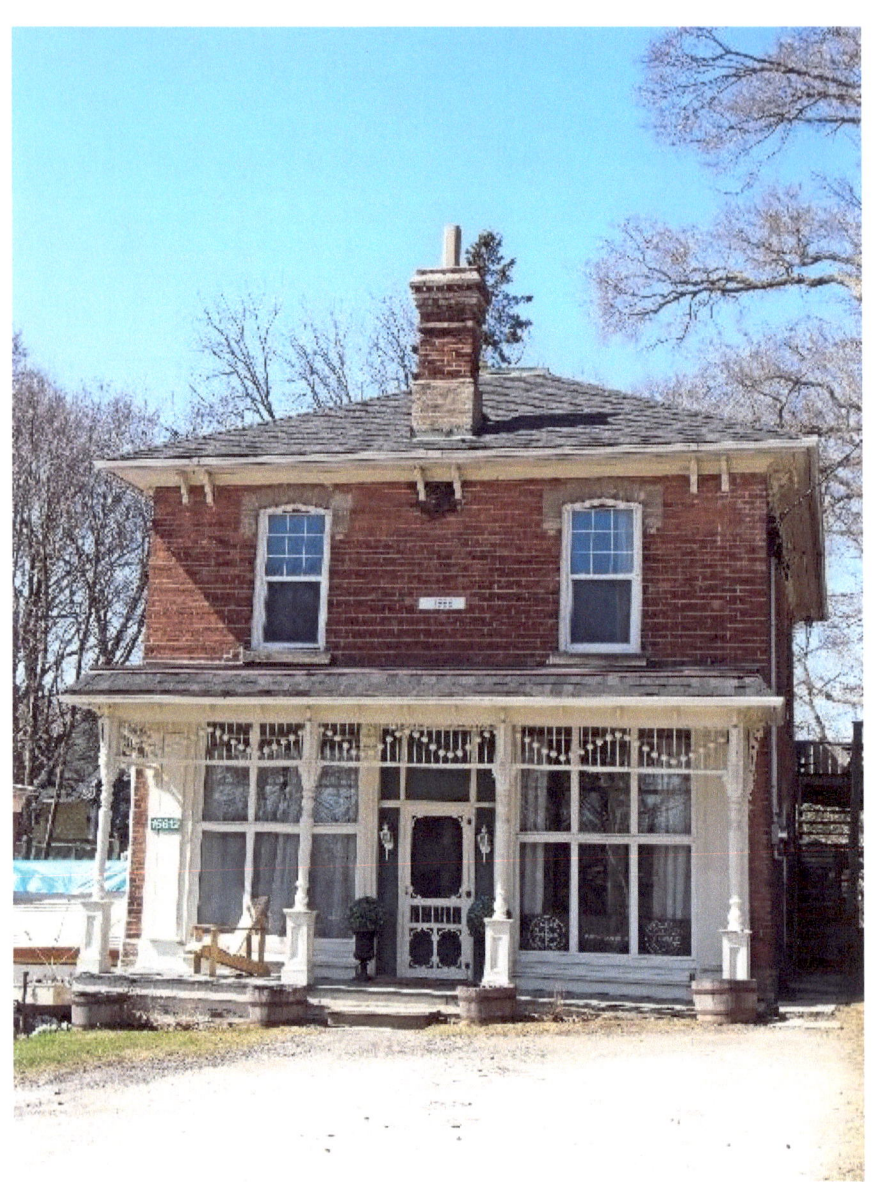

Belfountain and Inglewood Book - Inglewood - 15612 McLaughlin Road – General Store – 1886 - George Merry built this red brick, hip roofed general store and located a bake-oven at the rear. Note the date stone, brick façade, paired brackets and the verandah's decorative spool-work trim.

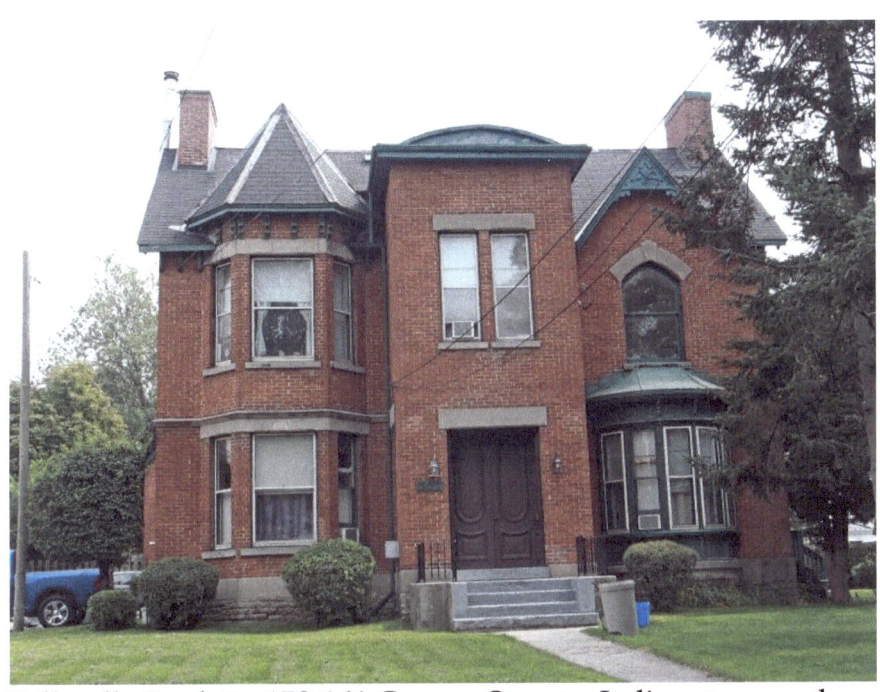

Belleville Book 1 - 159-161 George Street – Italianate – north side has a projecting two storey bay with a string course above the ground floor windows; south side has a projecting five window bay with carved wood paneling above it; window above has an arched lintel, two-storey frontispiece, gable with verge board trim – heritage property

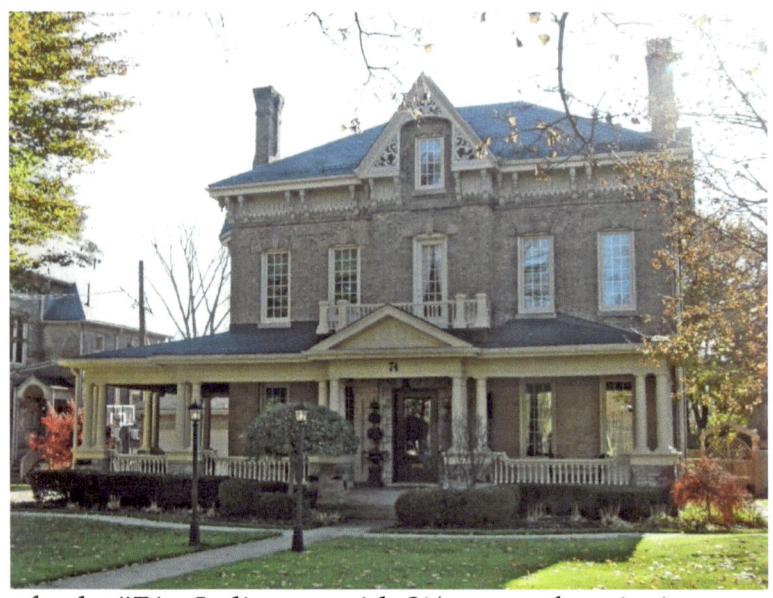

Brantford - #74 – Italianate with 2½ storey frontispiece, wraparound verandah, pediment, second floor balcony, verge board

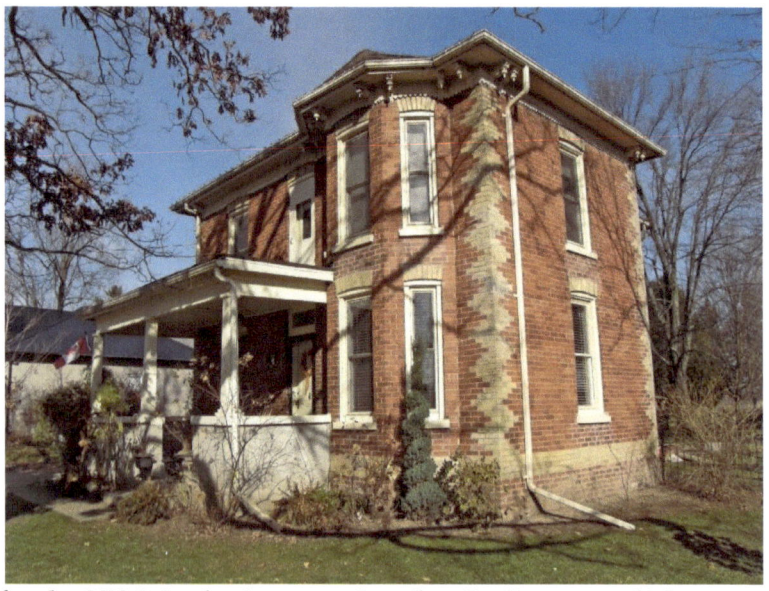

Burford - 358 Maple Avenue South – Italianate - dichromatic brickwork on corners

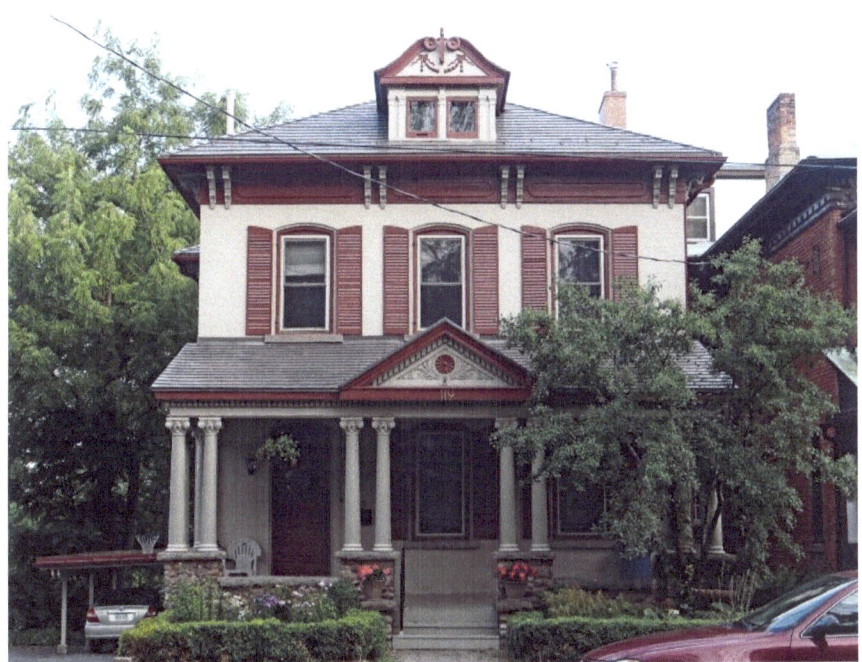

Brockville - 119 King Street East – Italianate - dormer with broken pediment and decorated tympanum; hipped roof; paired cornice brackets; composite pillars supporting veranda with pediment and decorative tympanum

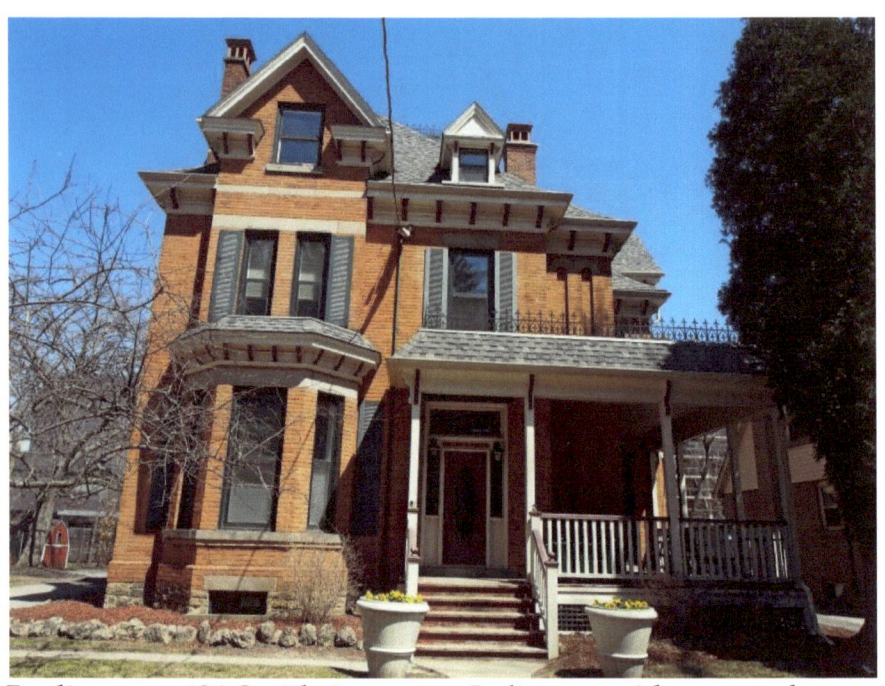

Burlington - 431 Smith Avenue – Italianate with two-and-a-half storey tower-like bay with cornice return on gable, dormer, single cornice brackets, bay window

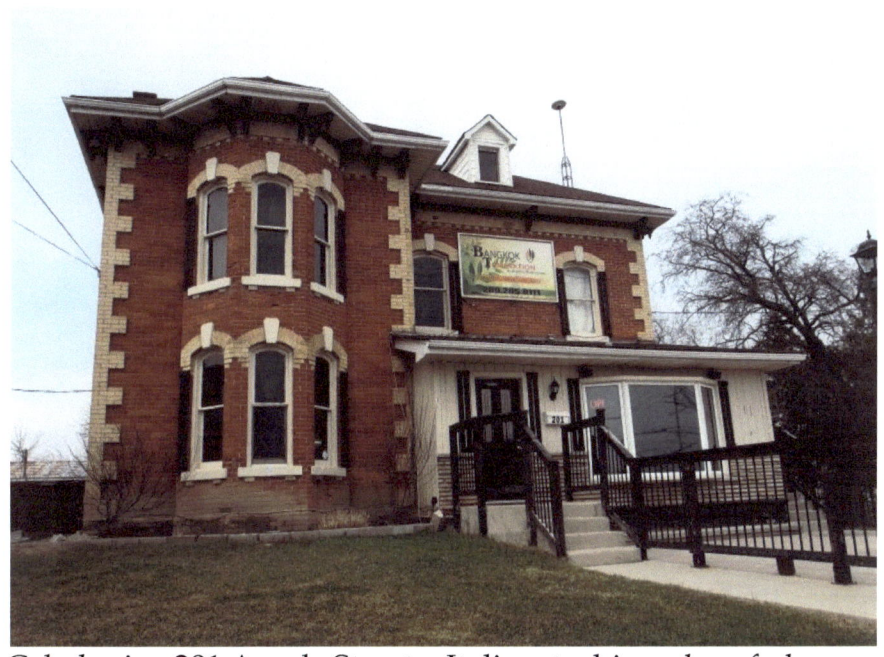

Caledonia - 201 Argyle Street – Italianate, hipped roof, dormer in attic, corner quoins, keystones and voussoirs, dichromatic brickwork, dentil moulding under cornice, paired brackets

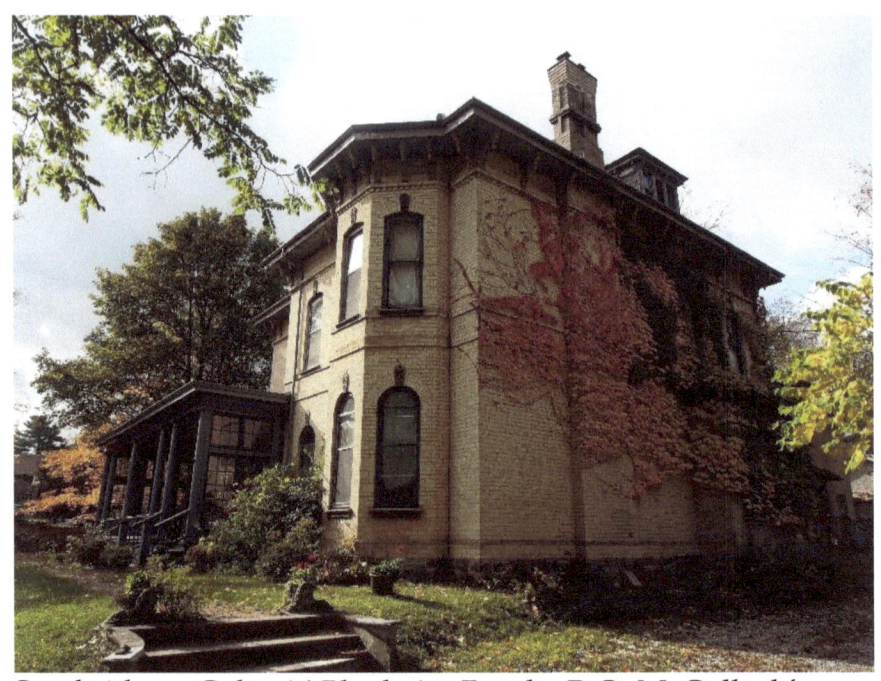

Cambridge – Galt - 16 Blenheim Road – R.O. McCulloch's House – c. 1879 – yellow brick, Italianate style – cornice brackets, dentil moulding, decorative concrete keystones, wooden logia-style porch

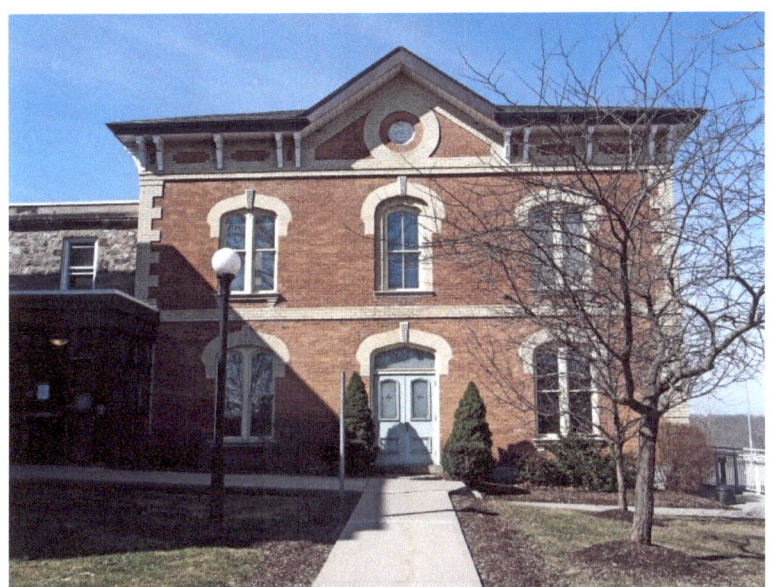

Cayuga - 55 Munsee Street – Jailer's Residence – 1877 – Italianate style, low hipped roof, overhanging eaves with brackets, a bullseye window

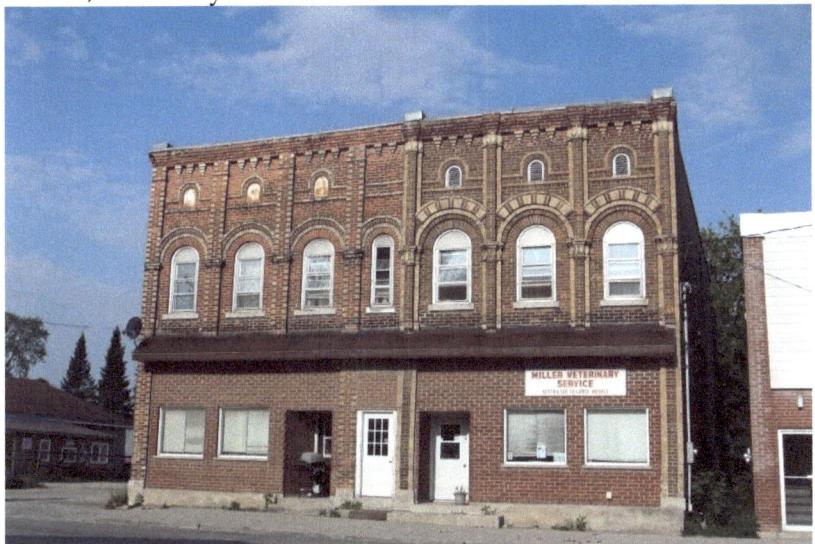

Chatsworth - 271 Garafraxa Street – Miller Veterinary Service – pilasters, dichromatic brickwork, voussoirs

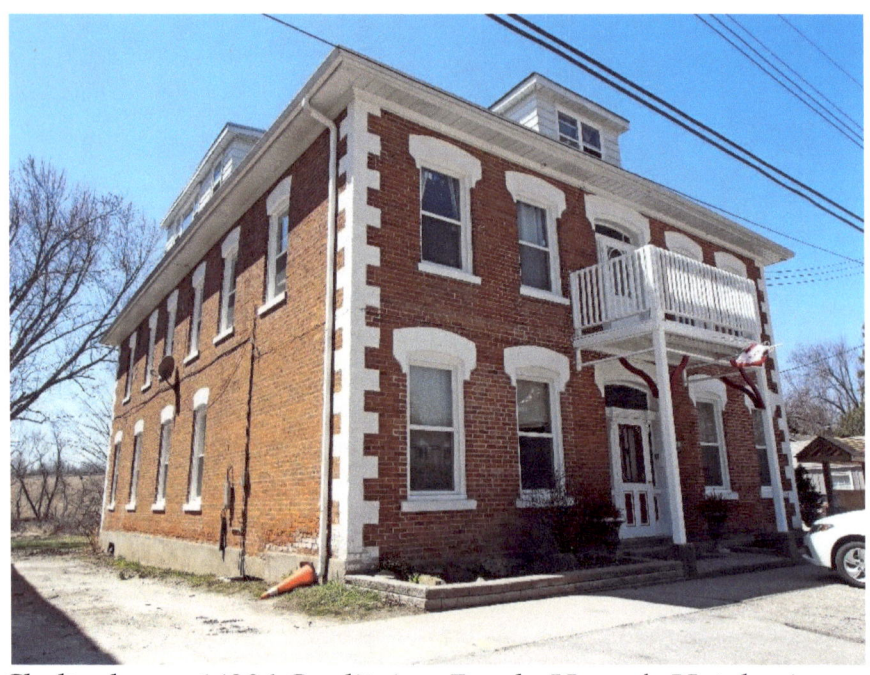

Cheltenham - 14396 Creditview Road - Henry's Hotel - circa 1887 - William Henry's pre-1859 Inn was destroyed in the 1887 fire. He rebuilt, replacing the Inn with this two-storey Georgian style frame building with hip roof and brick veneer. He named it 'Henry's Hotel' operating it until his death in 1904. Thomas and Nathaniel Browne took it over as 'Browne's Hotel'. It was later a butcher shop with home above. In 1958 it was adapted to commercial/apartment use.

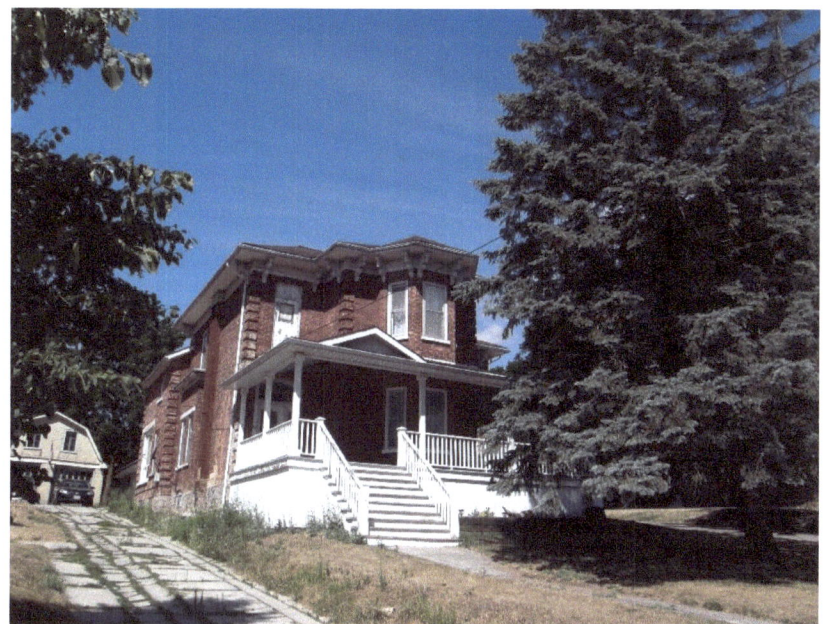

Chesley – hipped roof, cornice brackets, corner quoins, pediment

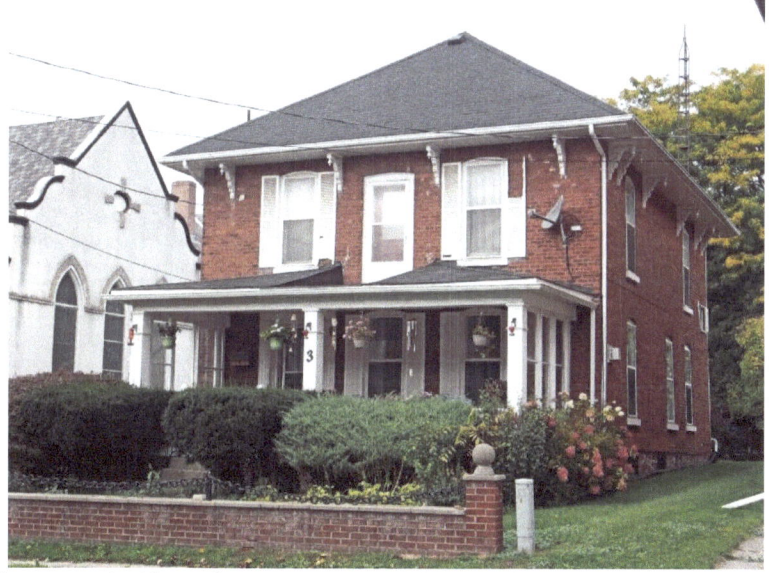

Colborne - 3 Church Street East – hipped roof, cornice brackets

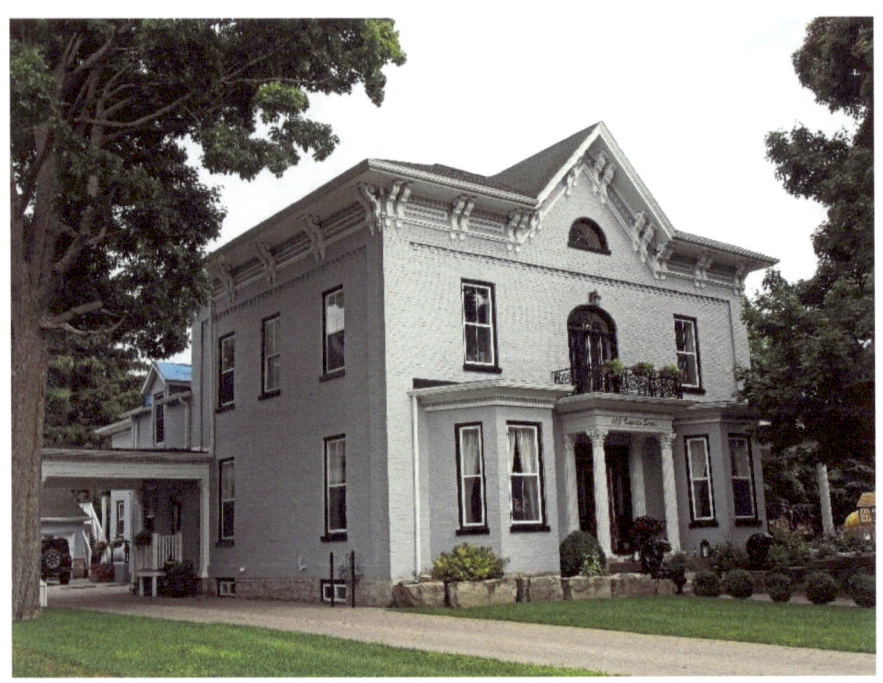

Cobourg Book 3 - 110 Ontario Street – 1878 – "Illahee Lodge" – Italianate – built by John Jeffrey, hardware merchant – bay windows, front porch crowned with intricate wrought iron railing

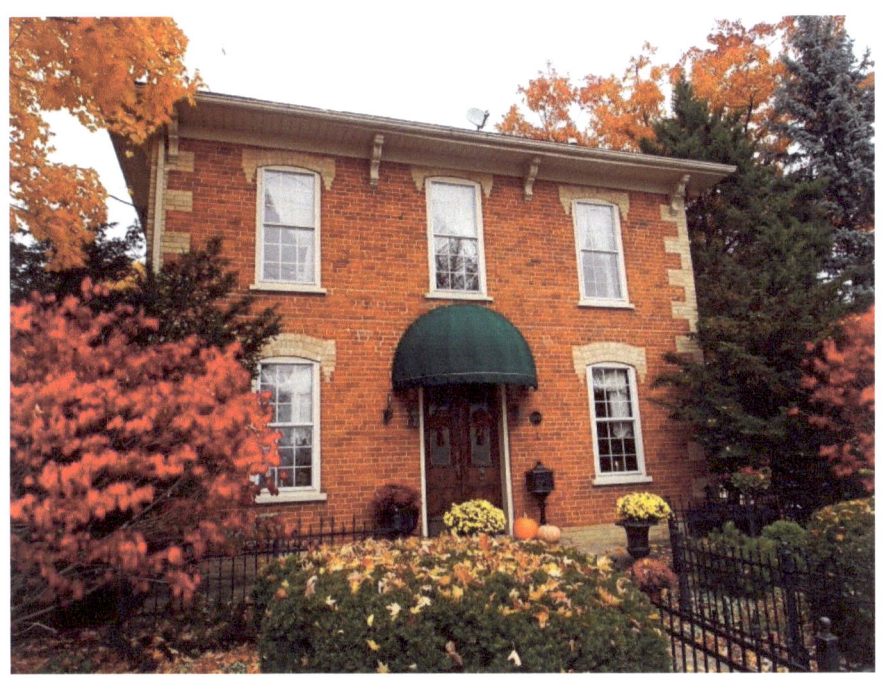

Conestogo - 1900 Sawmill Road - Italianate, corner quoins, single cornice brackets

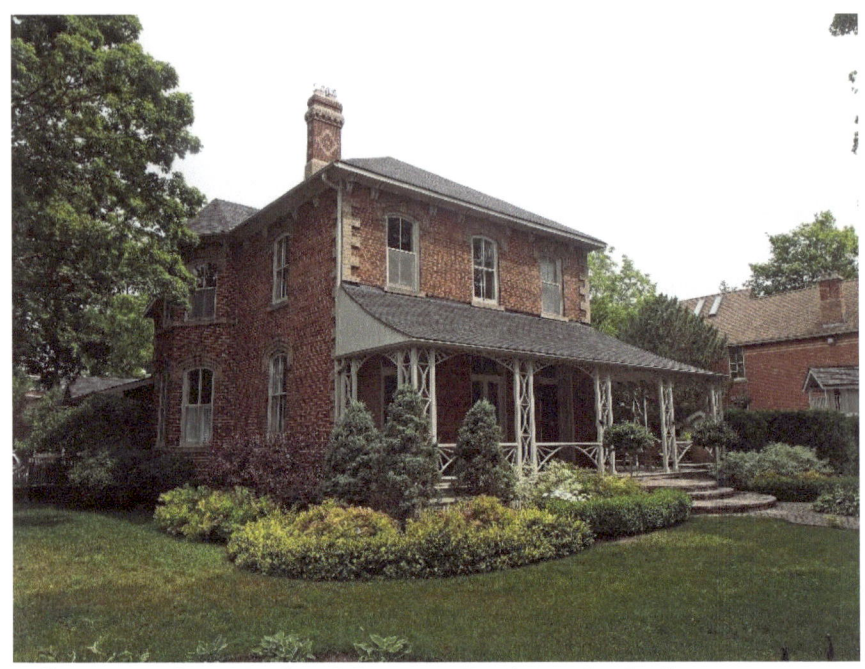

Collingwood - 199 Third Street – Built in the Italianate tradition for the Toner family, early coal and lumber merchants, this home has retained its elegance with minor alterations since 1882. The interior of the home features a circular staircase, marble fireplaces, plaster medallions and a built-in buffet. The exterior brick work laid in the common bond tradition is highlighted by protruding quoins and plinth in lighter contrasting brick. Decorative brick work adorns the original chimney as well as highlighting the window openings. Brick arch work and keystones decorate the window surrounds in a unique three-tiered stepped arch design. The main front façade contains unique, French doors with recessed mullion and molded panels. The home has a heavily bracketed low hip roof with an east side gable featuring a combination of corniced boxed brackets.

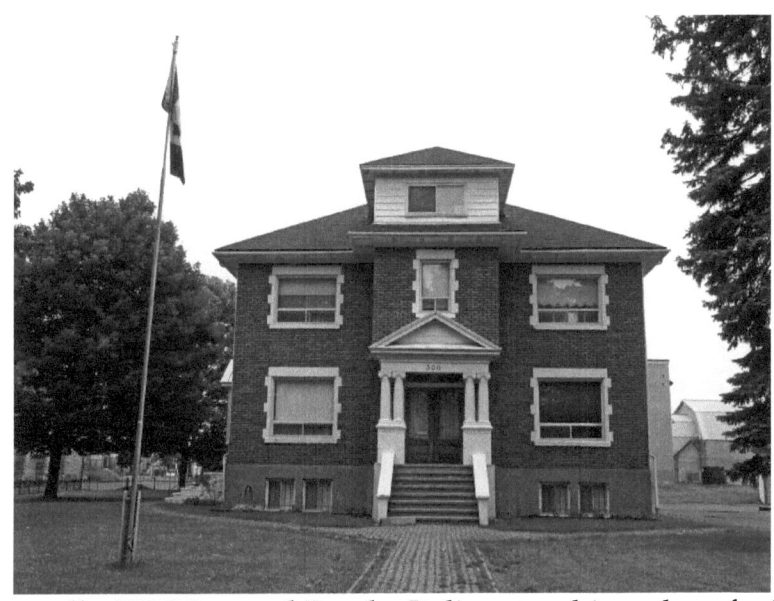

Cornwall - 300 Montreal Road – Italianate – hipped roof with dormer; pillars with Ionic capitals; pediment; quoining around windows

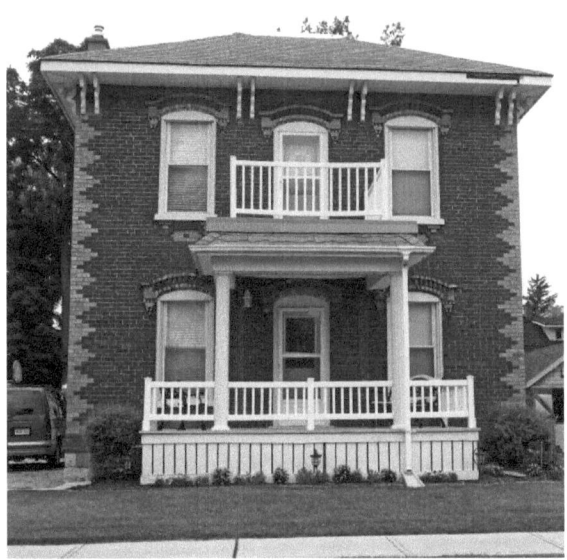

Delhi - Two-storey Italianate, paired cornice brackets, 2nd floor balcony, corner quoins, elegant voussoirs over windows and door

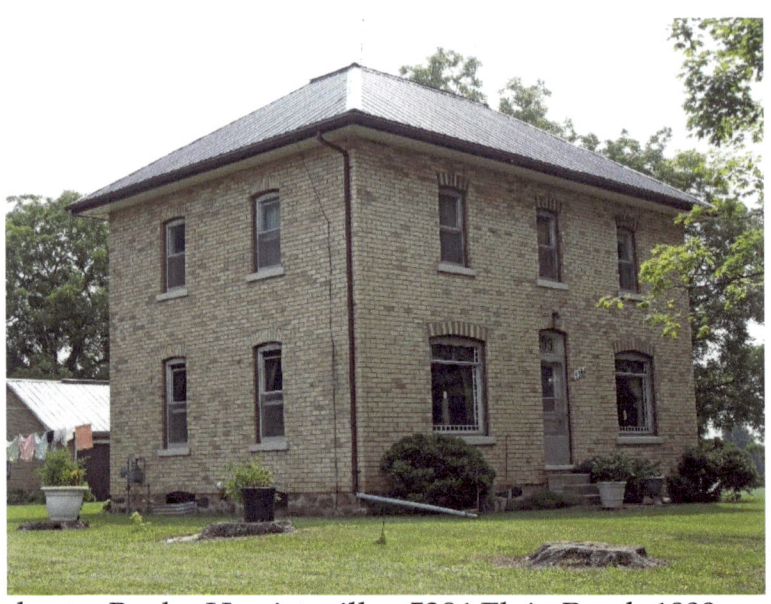

Dorchester Book - Harrietsville - 5384 Elgin Road -1899 – Italianate, hipped roof

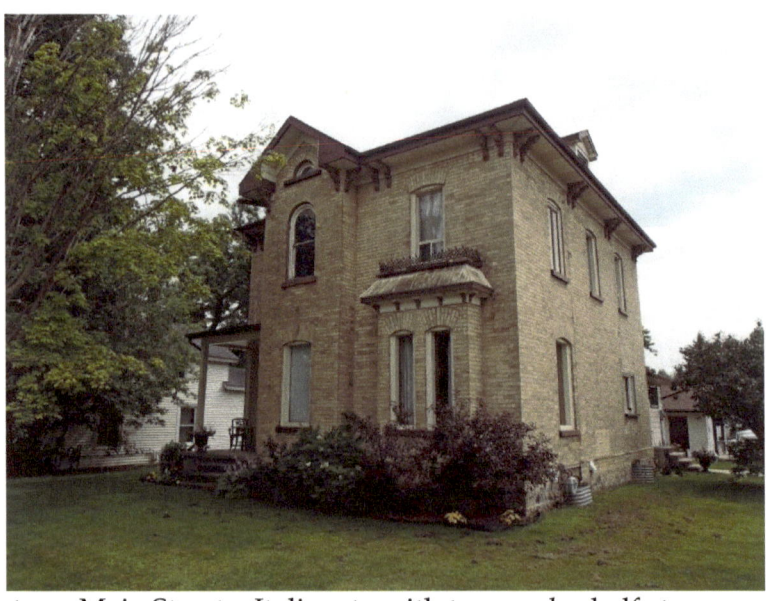

Drayton - Main Street – Italianate with two-and-a-half storey frontispiece, cornice brackets, bay window with iron cresting above

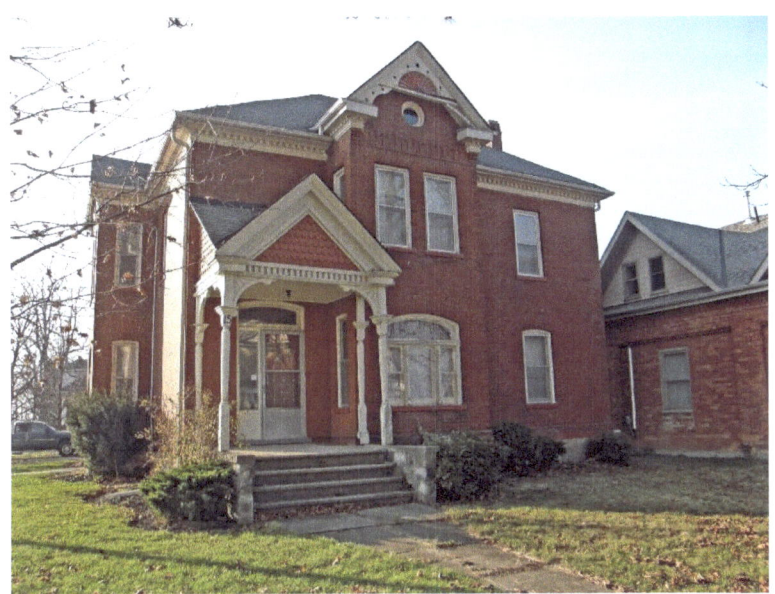

Drumbo Book - #15 – Italianate – verge board trim on gable, pediment

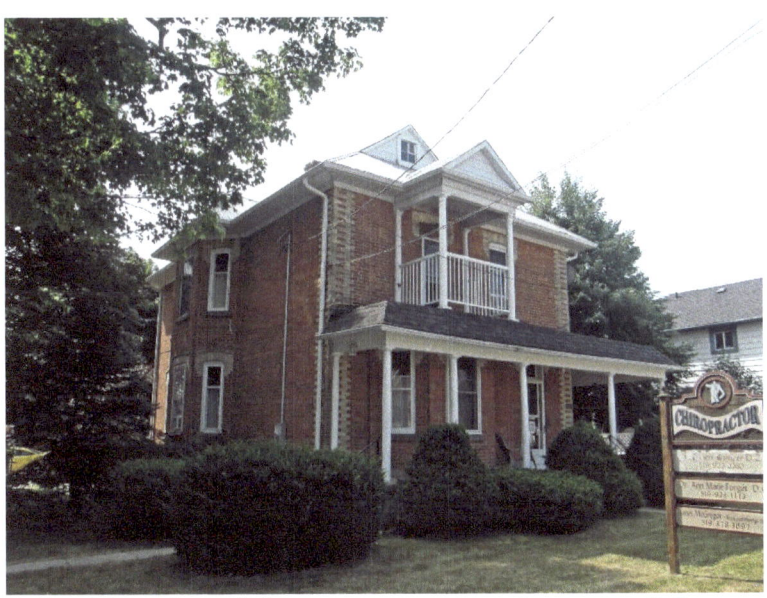

Dundalk – hipped roof, dormers, corner quoins, second-floor balcony

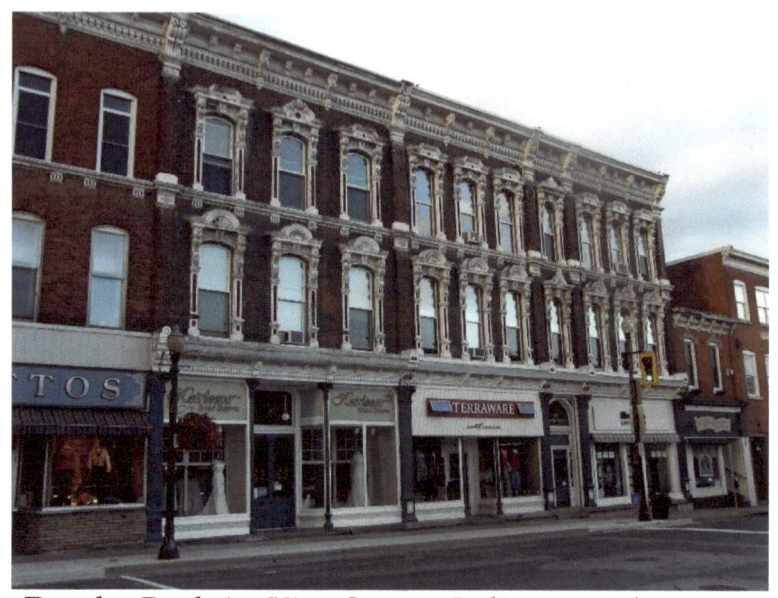
Dundas Book 1 – King Street - Italianate architecture

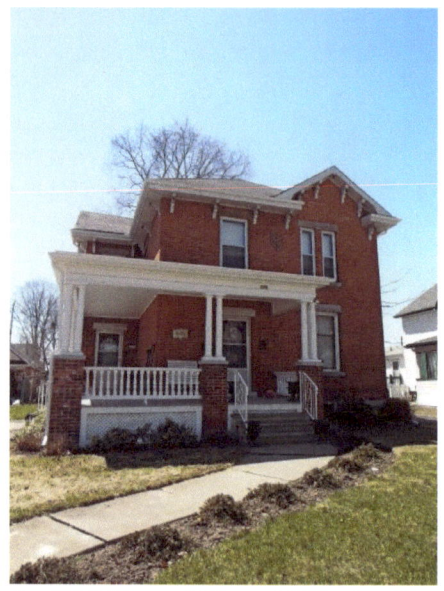
Dunnville Book 1 - 210 Broad Street West – Bartlett residence – c. 1901 - hipped roof, cornice brackets, wraparound veranda

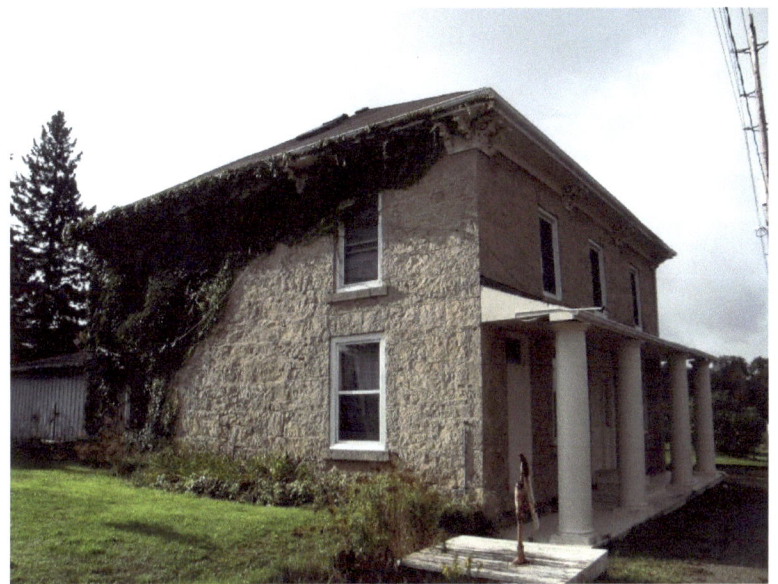

Eden Mills Book – Everton - stone building, cornice brackets, Doric pillars

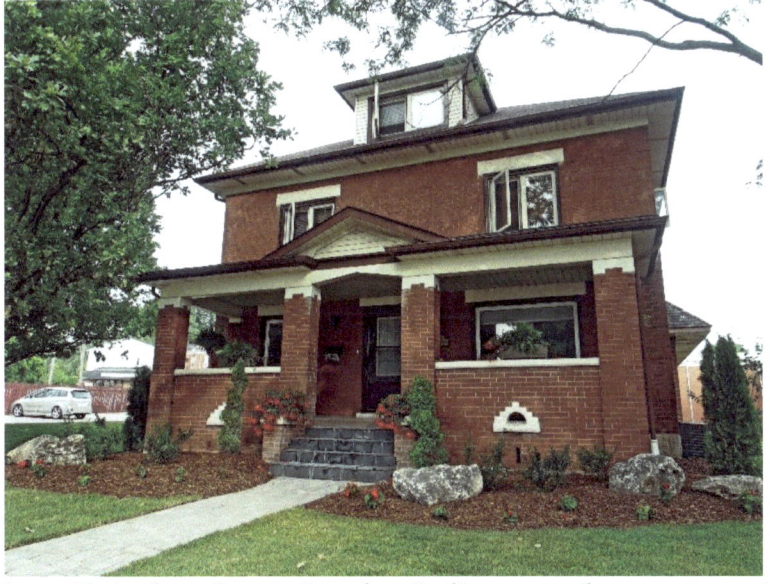

Elmira - 62 Arthur Street South – Italianate – dormer in attic

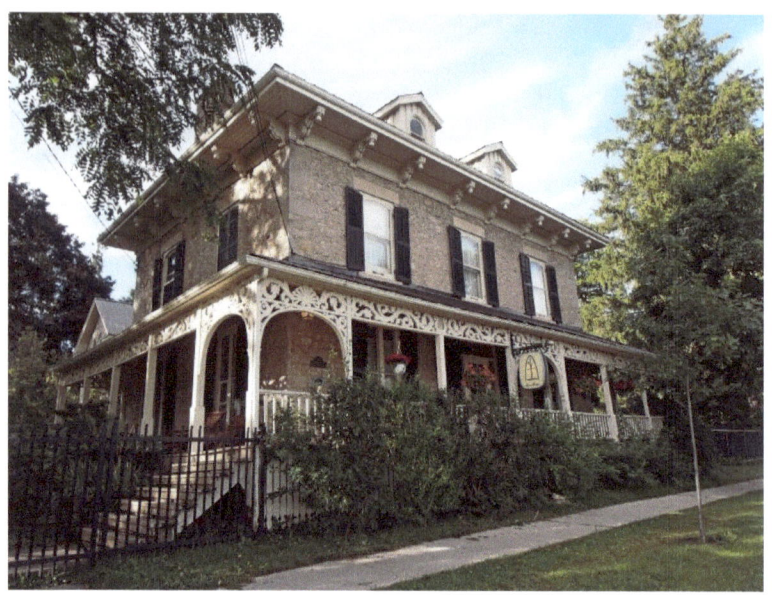

Elora - 120 Mill Street East – Drew House - Italianate style – dormers in attic, single cornice brackets, wraparound verandah with bric-a-brac

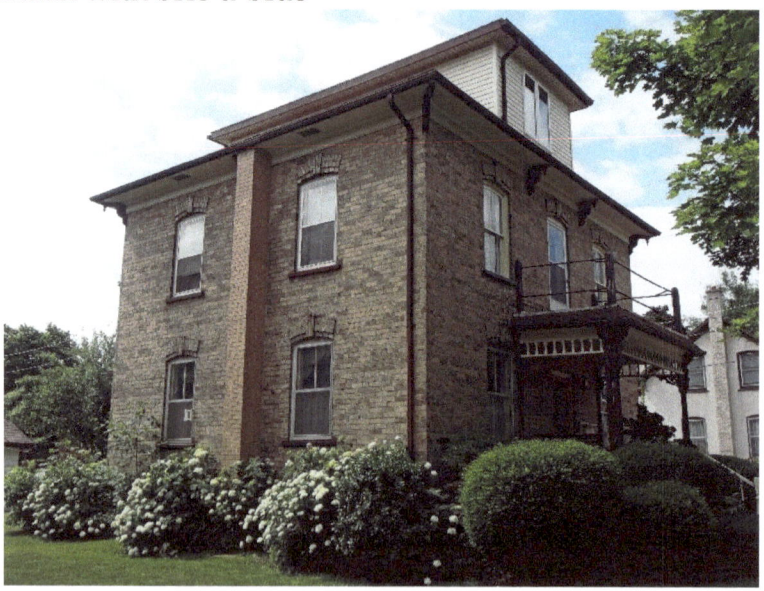

Elmira Book 1 - 31 Memorial Avenue – Italianate – dormer in attic, cornice brackets

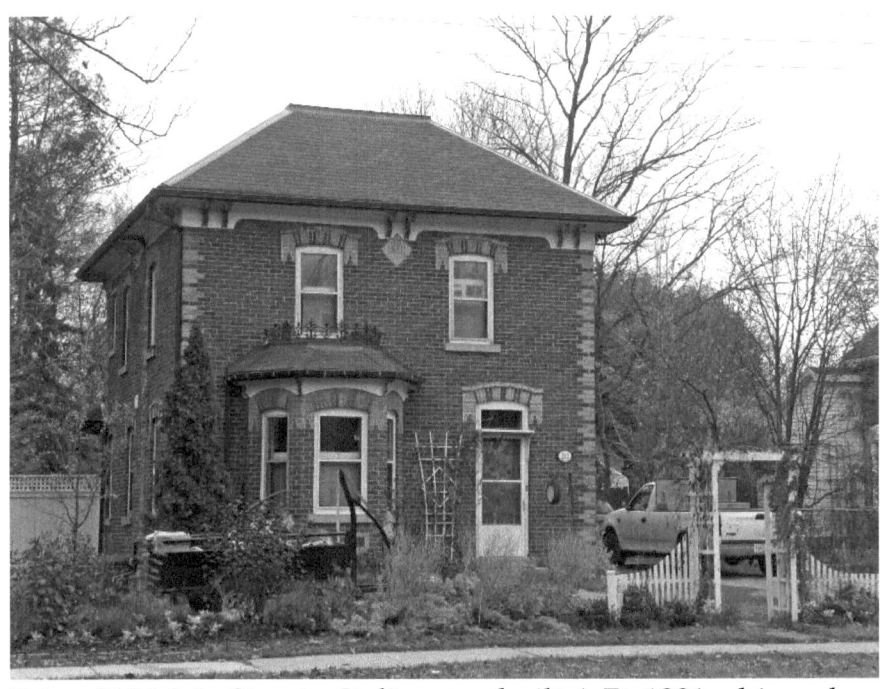

Erin - 213 Main Street – Italianate - built A.D. 1891 – hipped roof, paired cornice brackets, iron cresting above bay window, dichromatic brickwork

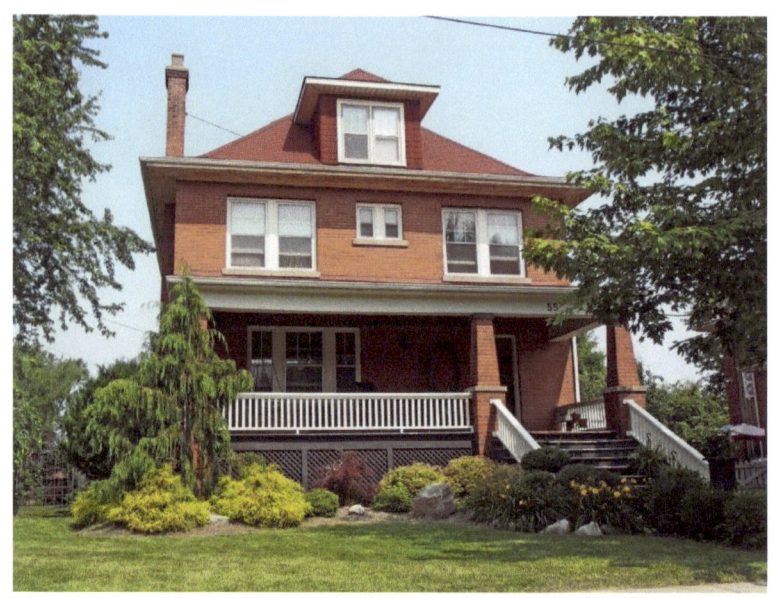

Essex - 55 Centre Street – Italianate, hipped roof, dormer

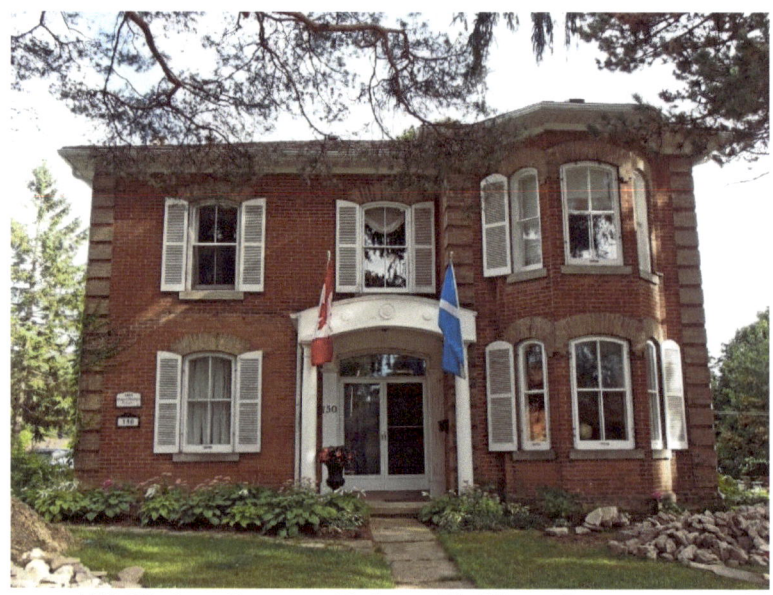

Fergus - 150 Union Street – Robert Phillips, Druggist c. 1883 - Italianate, hipped roof, corner quoins, two-storey tower-like bay

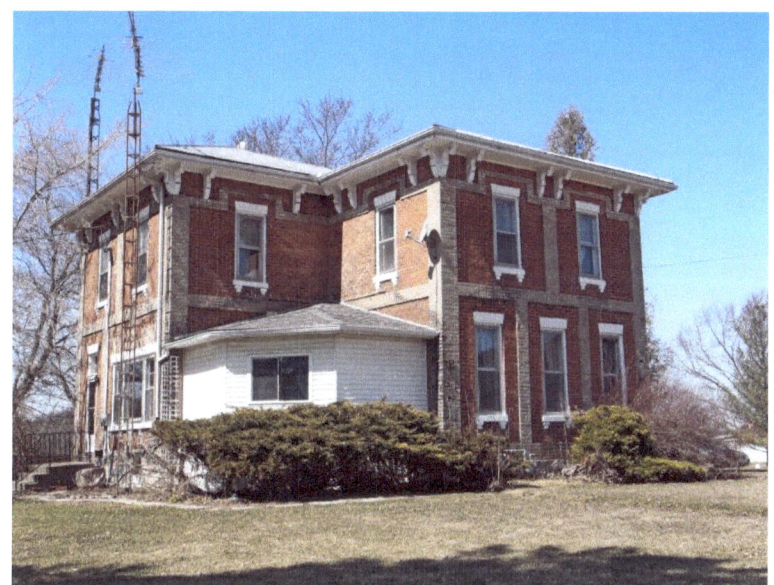

Fisherville Book – Selkirk - 15 Erie Street North – Italianate, hipped roof, cornice brackets, quoins, banding

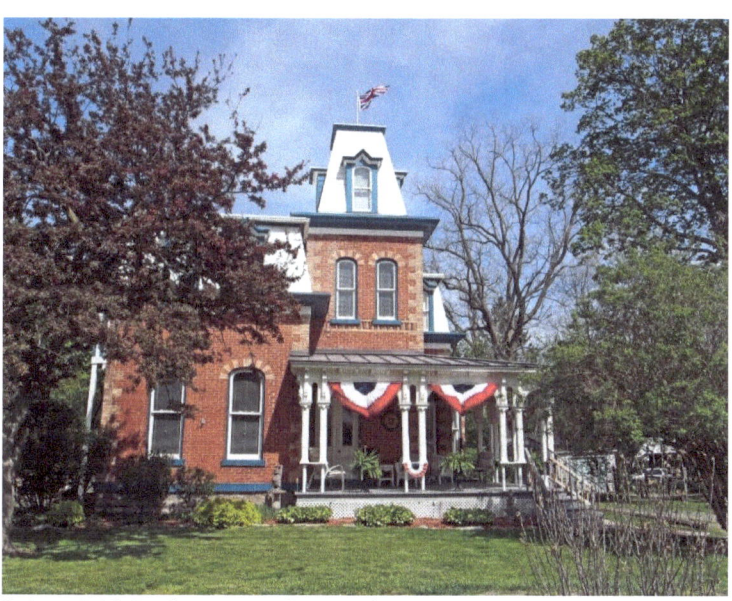

Fort Erie - 348 Ridge Road North

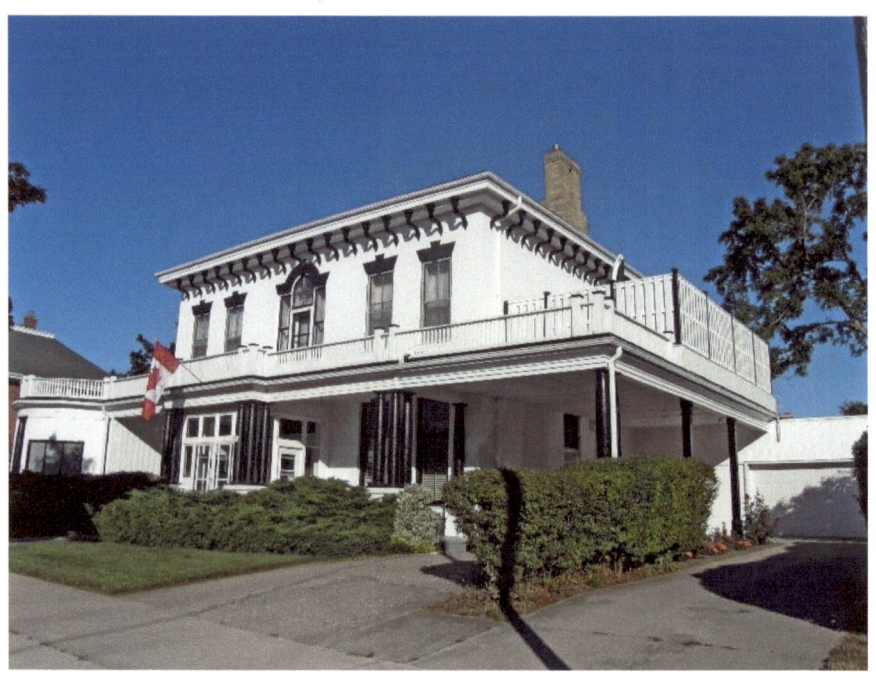

Goderich - 65 Montreal Street – The "Garrow House" was built around 1850 and was the residence of James Thompson Garrow who later became Supreme Court Judge and local Judge of the Canadian Exchequer Court. It is in the Italianate style with unusual bracketing, a two-storey veranda, large front windows and two end chimneys, a central Palladian window and decorative stone lintels and keystones.

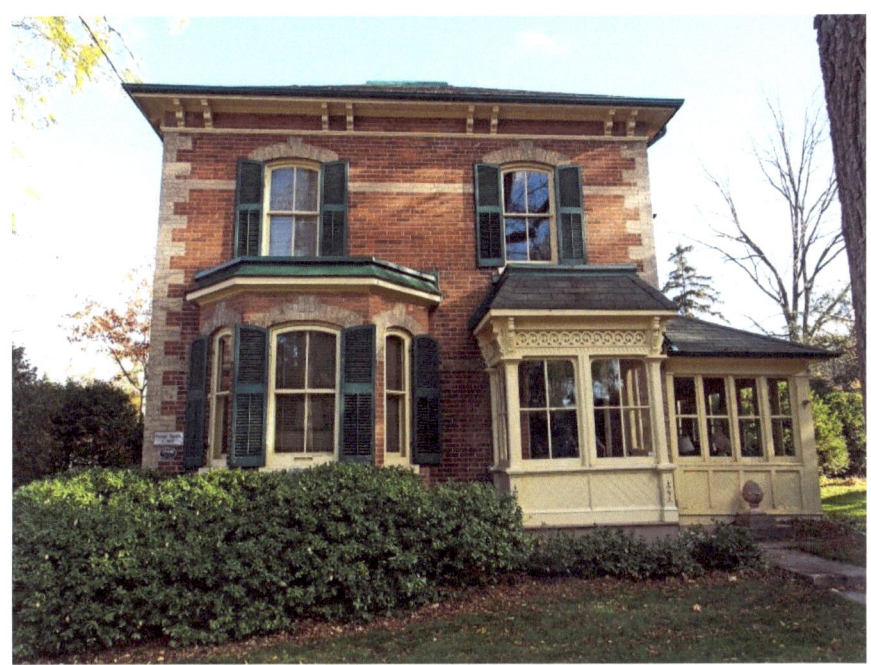

Grafton Bolton Book – Bolton - 31 Nancy Street - *George Smith House - circa 1877 - This Italianate style home was built by George Watson for Margaret and George Smith. The red and yellow bricks were locally made and its exterior architectural features and beautiful enclosed porches are original. Smith, a sign painter and letterer, sat on the first village Council and was noted for his very realistic interior faux-wood graining. Erie Smith Schaefer inherited the house in 1933, living here with her husband Alex of 'Smith & Schaefer' Hardware. This dichromatic brick house is in the Italianate style. The orientation of the 'L' plan with the enclosed verandah along the south is distinctive. The bracketed eaves, segmentally arched windows and low medium pitch hipped roof are all typical of the Italianate.

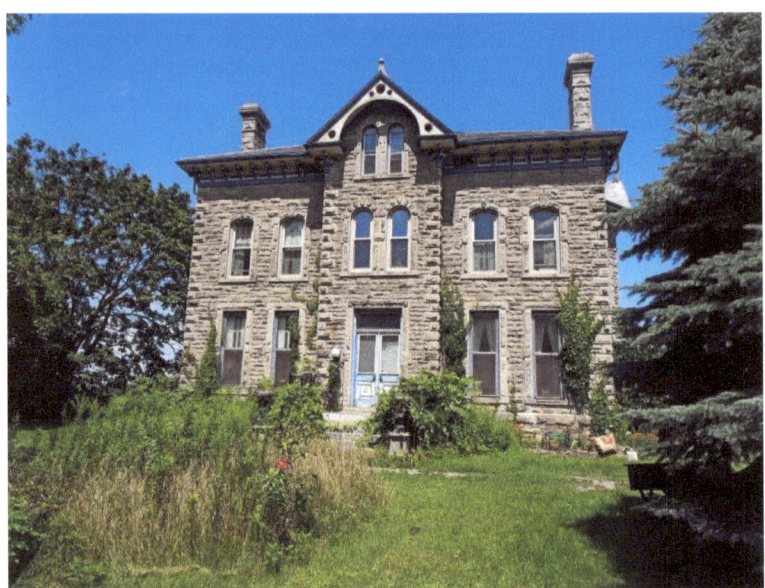

Grimsby - 390 Main Street West – names for the house are Smith-Geddes House, Thornfield Hall, The Stone House - The two-and-a-half-storey stone building was constructed between 1876 and 1878. The Smith-Geddes House was built on a flat area of land amidst orchards of peach and cherry trees. The rural location, close to Lake Ontario to the northeast and the Niagara escarpment to the southwest, creates a unique natural setting.

This house is an important example of a high-Victorian country house in the Italianate architectural style rendered in a vernacular form. The stone house has a five-bay façade with a projecting frontispiece, containing the main entrance of wood paneled doors, a transom of colored glass and the etched initials of John Henry Smith. Paired round-headed windows above the center door and a smaller pair on the third floor are under a projecting gable, with a carved-wood verge board.

The hip, patterned-slate roof has corniced edges of wood brackets, supporting the soffit. Four chimneys of quarry-faced stone, laid in random ashlar, project from each corner of the house and are decorated with pediment moldings along the stacks. The two flanking bays of the main façade have pairs of square-headed windows on the first floor and segmented arches on the second. The stone work is quarry-faced ashlar with projecting rusticated quoins and window surrounds. A projecting wing on the west side is capped with a gable. A wide bay window with a gable roof projects from the east side.

The interior is laid out in a center-hall plan with an ornate wood staircase. The interior woodwork is walnut and oak, with carved mantels in both the east parlor and the dining room. The hallway and stairs are paneled in cherry. The wood windows have louvered shutters that fold into reveals matching the paneling of the windows and detailed baseboards are found throughout. The hall, east parlor and dining room have plaster moldings and plaster ceiling medallions. Elaborate cast-iron grills surround the radiators in each of the rooms. The original porch has been removed and a number of small additions have been made to the rear of the house, including a fire escape.

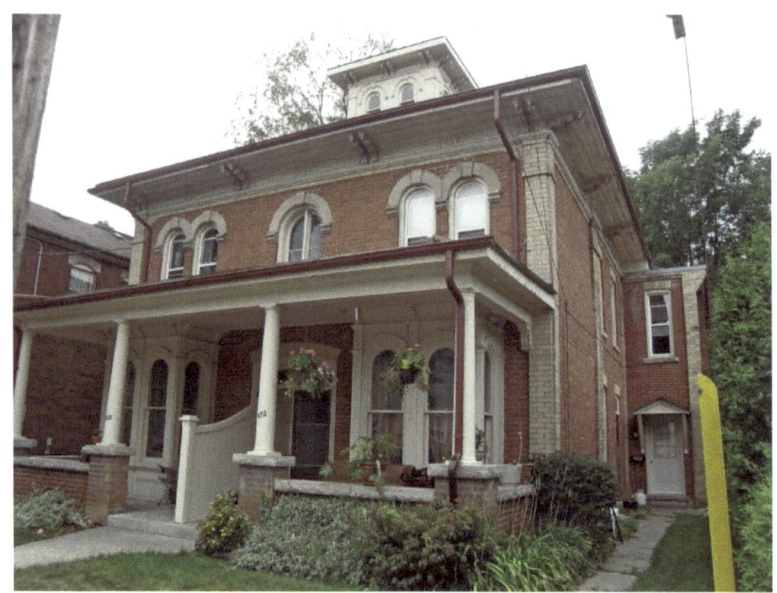

Guelph Book 1 - #430/432 – Italianate, arched window lintels with keystones, dormer in attic, decorative cornice, paired brackets, pilasters on corners and sides

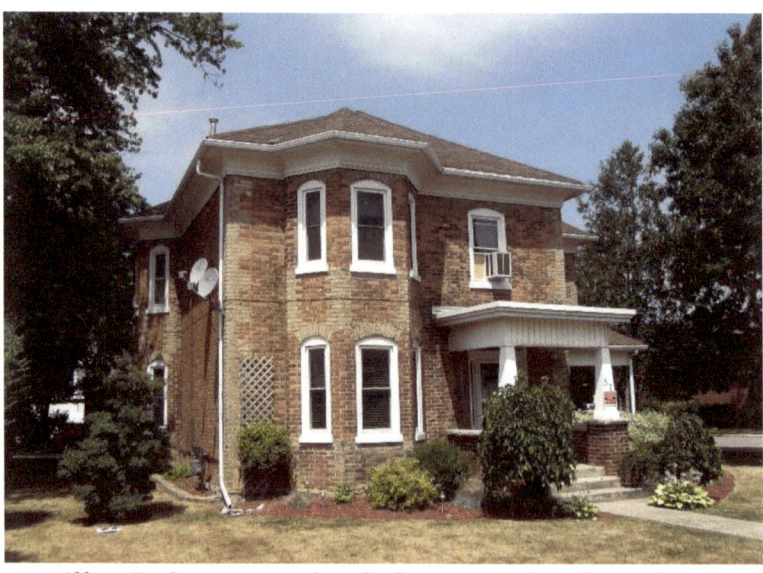

Hagersville - Italianate style, dichromatic brickwork, two-storey bay window

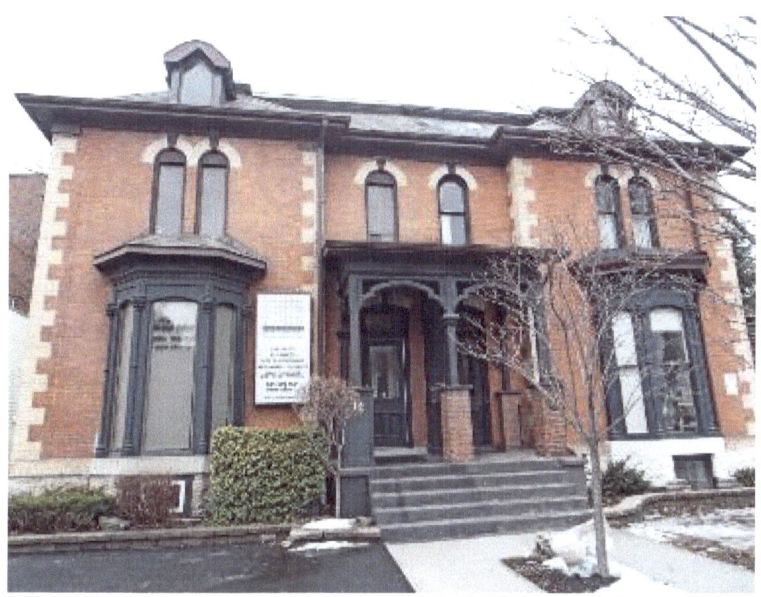

Hamilton Book 1 - 10-12 Ray Street – Italianate, dormers, corner quoins, keystones and voussoirs, bay windows

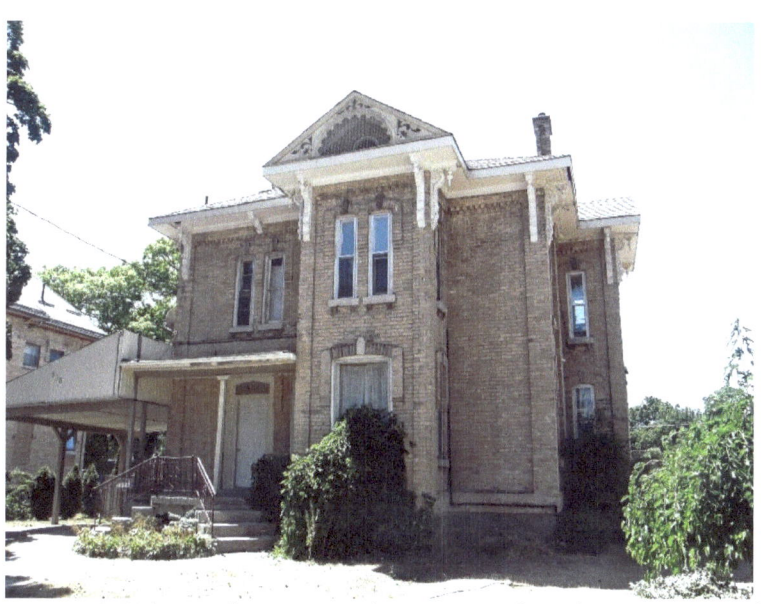

Hanover - #512 – Italianate style, cornice brackets, two-and-a-half storey tower-like bay with decorative gable

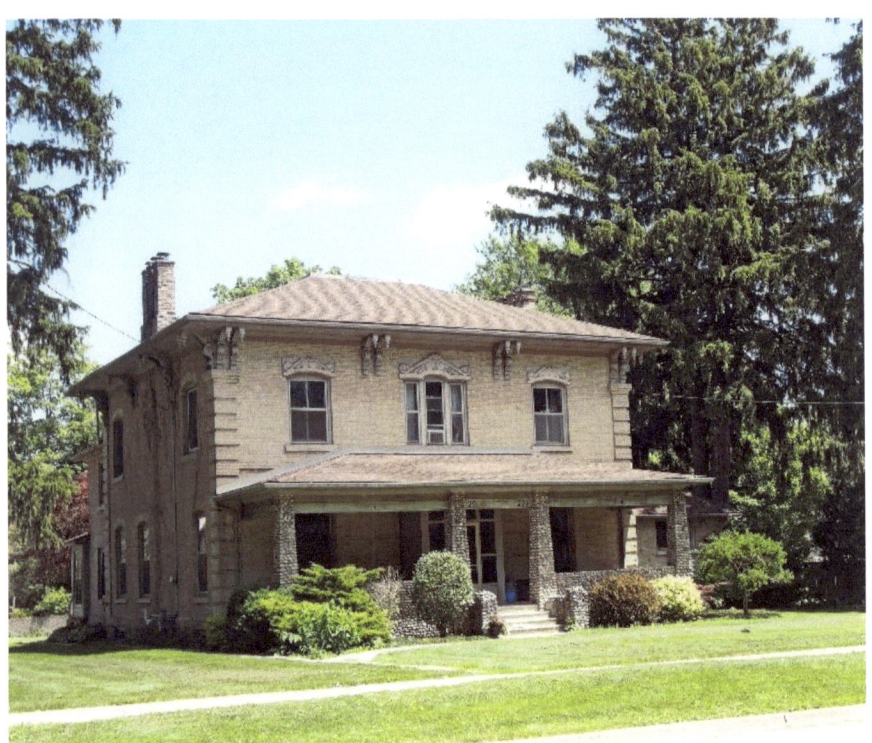

Ingersoll Book 1 - 291-293 Oxford Street – This home was built around 1880 and illustrates the typical broad bracketed eaves of the Italianate style. Fred J. Stone was one of the earliest occupants of this yellow brick house. He joined Wm. Stones Sons Ltd. in 1907 as manager of the Ingersoll branch. The operation started as a hide and wool business but soon developed into a fertilizer plant, later expanding to make livestock feed concentrates. In the 1920s, it passed into the possession of W.A.C. Forman, a family relative. At this time the house was divided to accommodate two units. His father owned the "FAIR", a store at 126 Thames St. South which sold dry goods and household furnishings and utensils. When the store came under the management of Mr. Forman Jr., it became known as "Forman's Set - $1.00". It has a hipped roof, paired cornice brackets, and corner quoins.

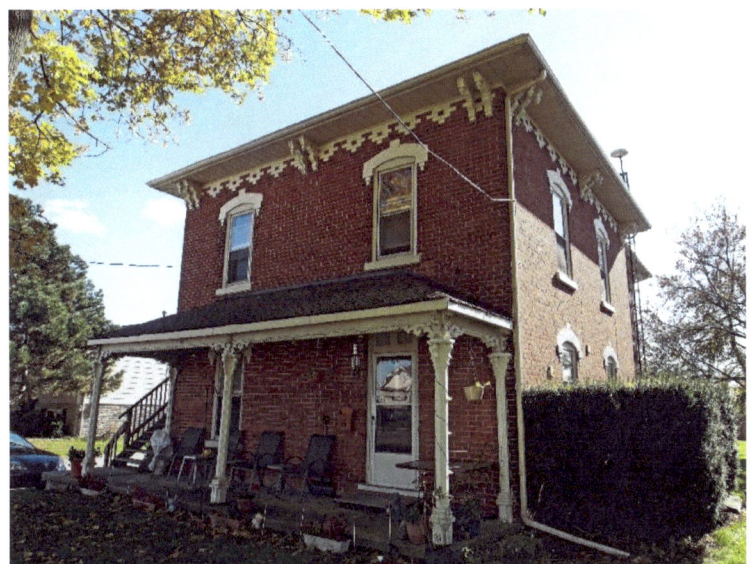

Jarvis - 53 Talbot Street – Italianate style, paired cornice brackets, dichromatic patterning below cornice, arched window hoods

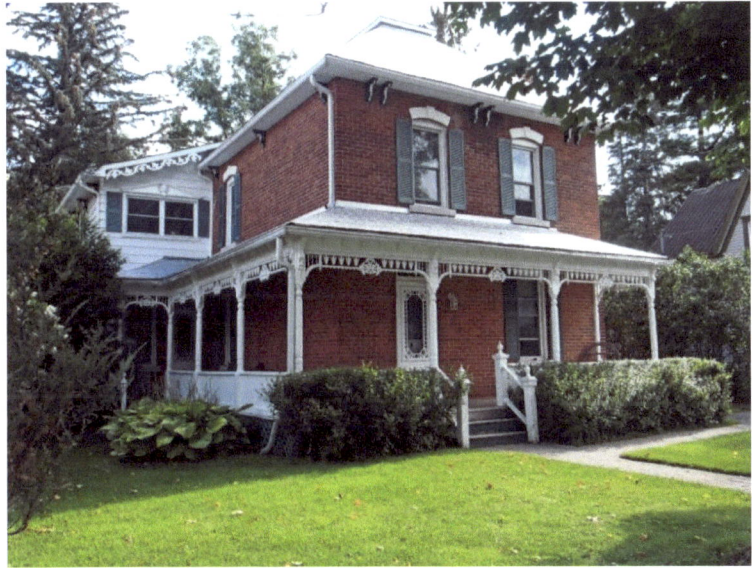

Kemptville - Prescott Street – Italianate - open wooden veranda with decorative support posts and open railings; hipped roof; paired cornice brackets; keystones above upper windows

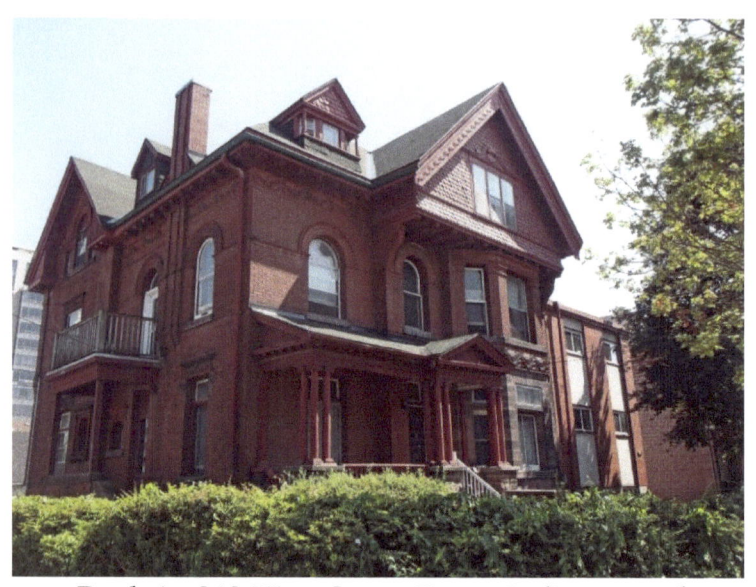

Kingston Book 1 - 213 King Street East – Italianate – decorative brickwork below cornice and above first floor windows, dormers with fish scale pattern in the gables, pediment, columns with Ionic capitals supporting the verandah

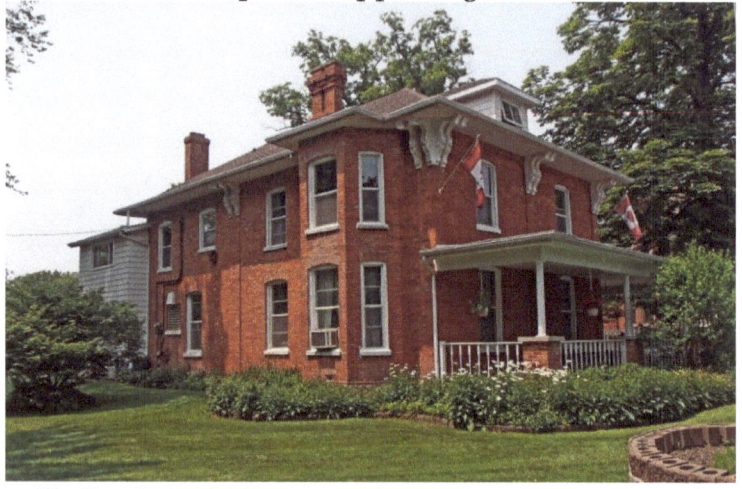

Kingsville Book 1 - 86 Division Street South – 2-storey brick house built in 1882 in the Italianate style, hipped roof, paired cornice brackets, dormer, cut fieldstone foundation, three large brick chimneys

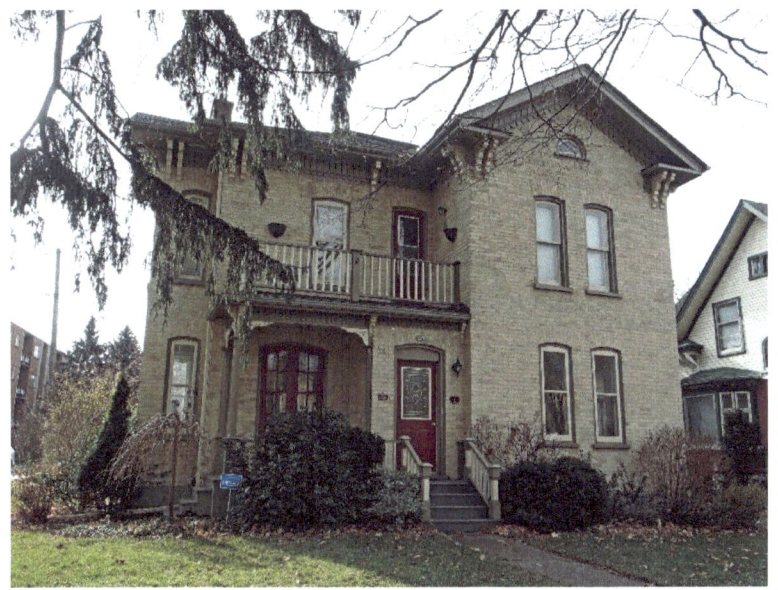

Kitchener Book 1 - 43 David Street – c. 1888 – Italianate with two-and-a-half storey tower-like bay with gable; ornate cornice brackets – yellow brick

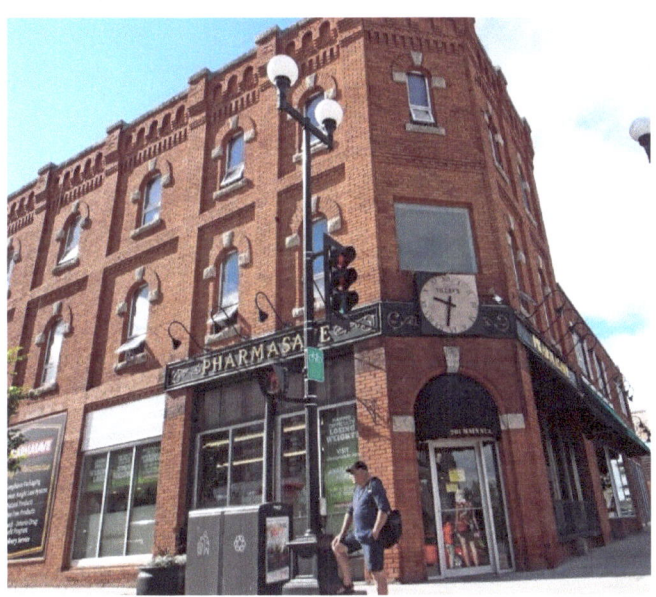

Lake Superior Book – Kenora - 201 Main Street South, - dentil molding, pilasters, voussoirs and keystones

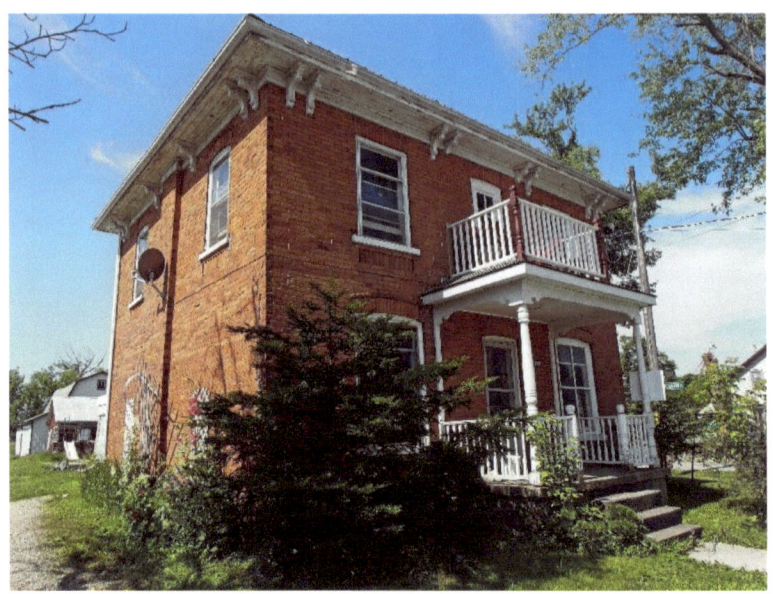
Linwood - 5106 Ament Line – Italianate, cornice brackets

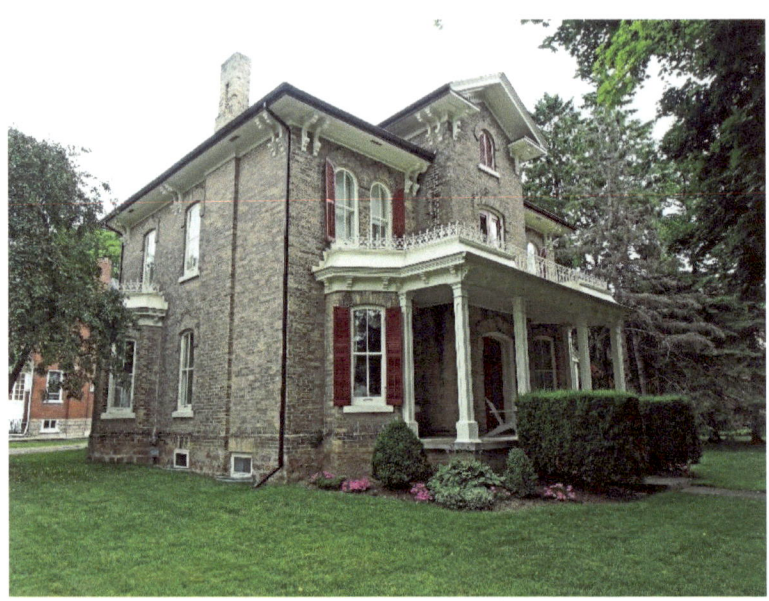
Listowel - 185 Binning Street West – Italianate with two-and-a-half storey tower-like bay, paired cornice brackets, balcony on second floor, cornice return on gable, built in 1872

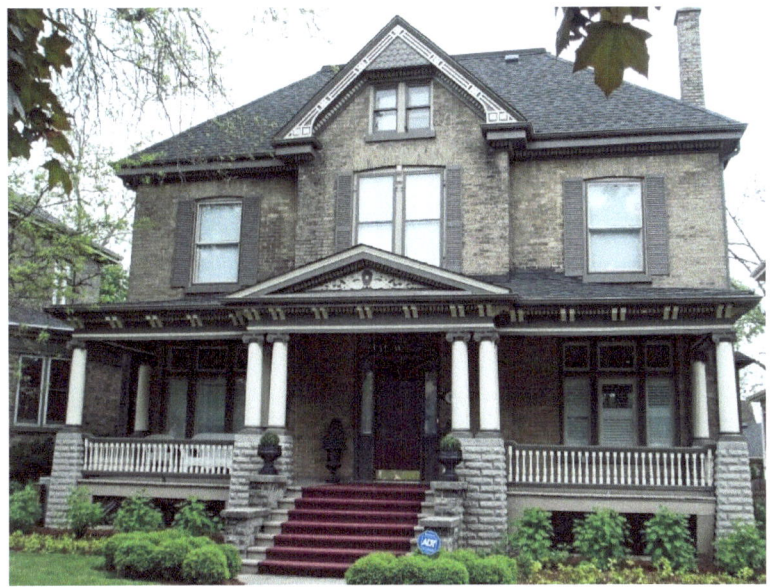

London - Italianate style with two-and-a-half storey tower-like bay, pediment above verandah

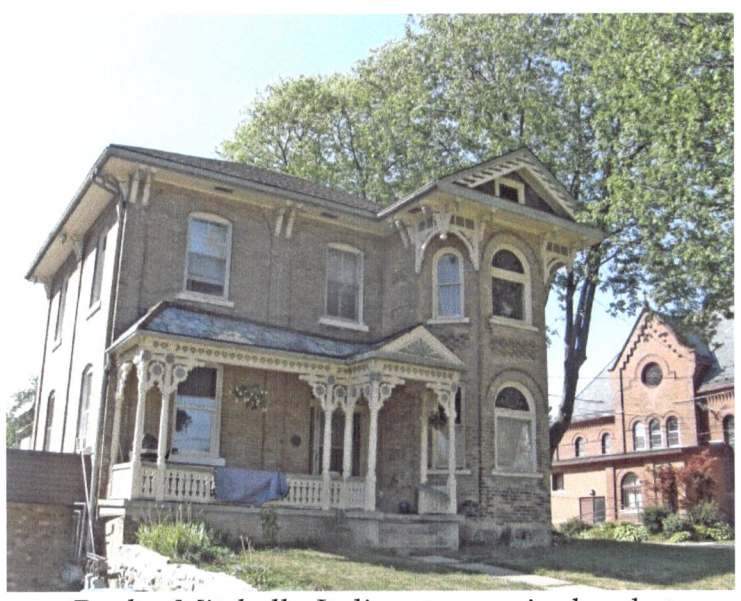

Lucknow Book – Mitchell - Italianate, cornice brackets, fretwork, decorative pillars on porch and pediment, 2½ storey tower-like bay

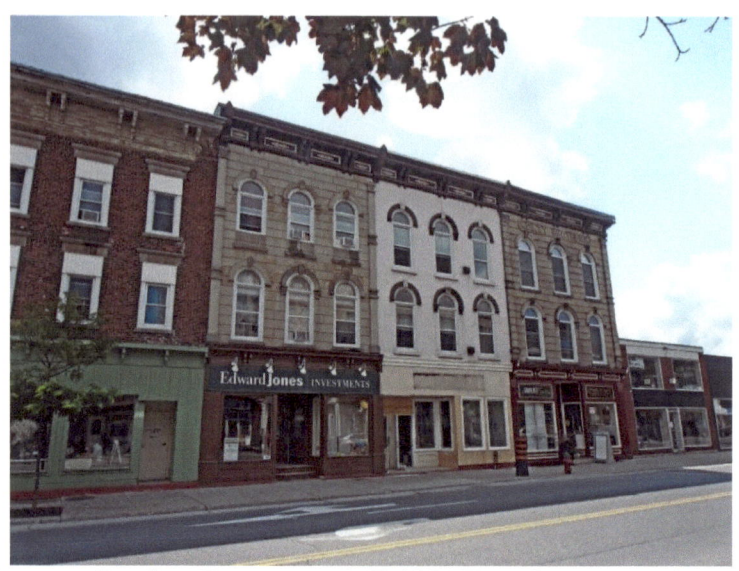

Mariatown Book – Prescott - 115-123 King Street - Italianate – 1874 – Keilty Block (Stern Building) - stone-on-brick façade, limestone round-headed windows, flat roof, decorative cornice, pilasters, keystones - facade uses different building materials to divide the block into three equal sections

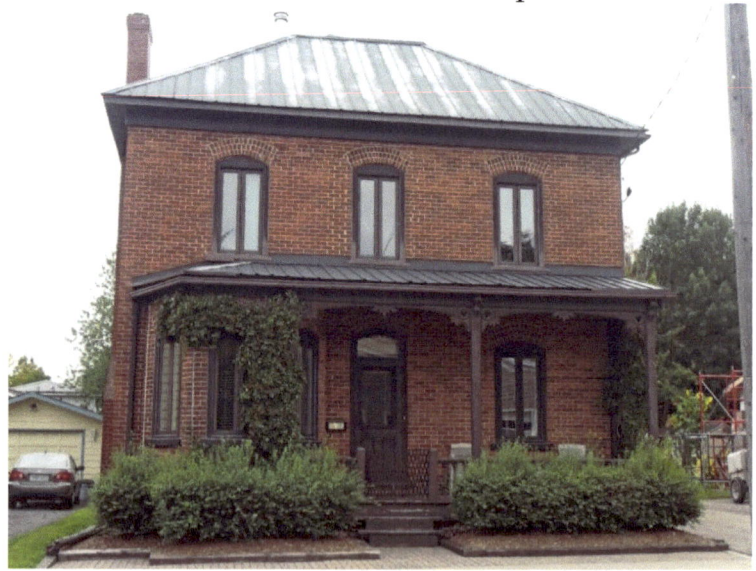

Merrickville - 511 St. Lawrence Street – hip roof

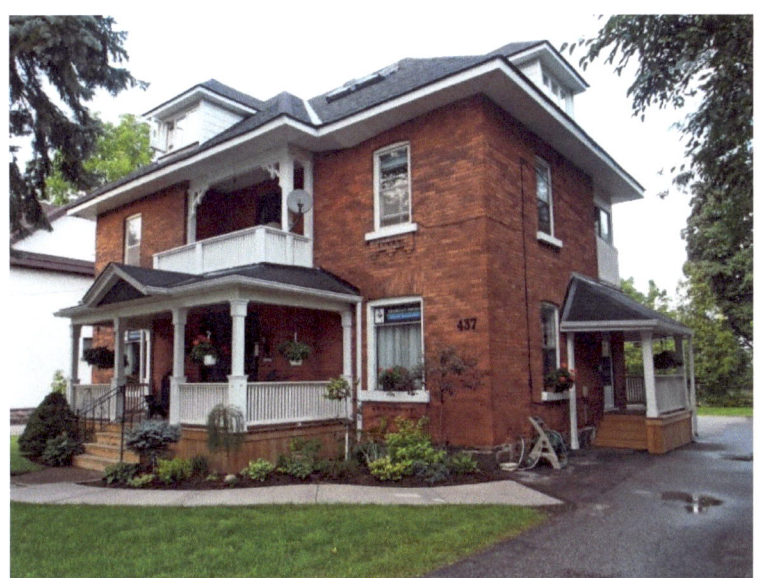

Midland - 437 King Street - exterior is stretcher brick with a cut stone foundation; medium hipped roof and two second storey balconies; brick voussoirs; decorative brick below some windows; sidelights; open verandah with open railings and wood piers

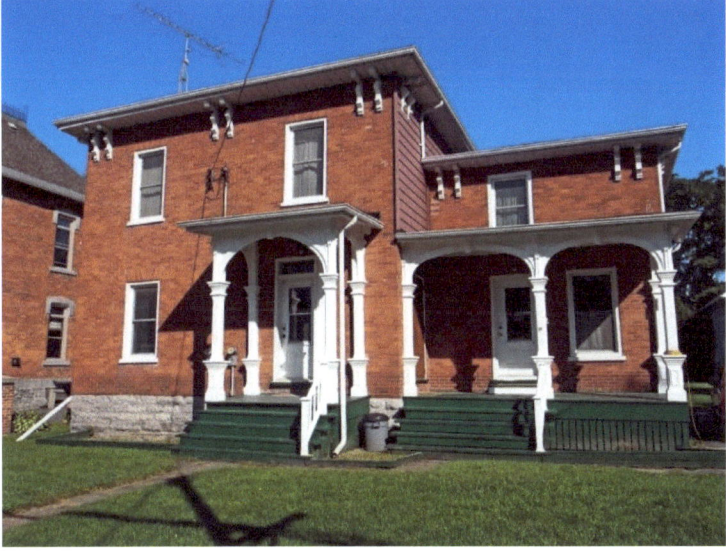

Morrisburg - 48 Lakeshore Drive – Italianate, paired cornice brackets, decorative porch and verandah supports; transom

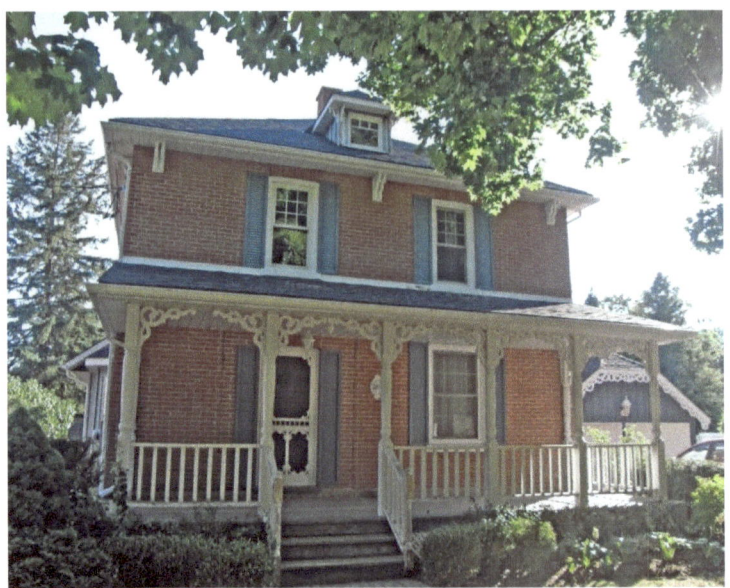

Mount Forest - #267 – Italianate, dormer in attic

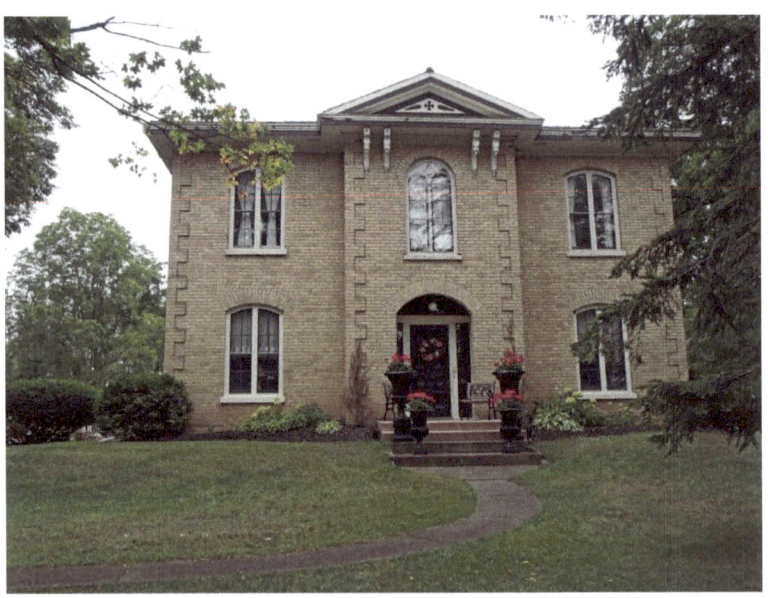

Mount Pleasant - 849 Mount Pleasant Road – circa 1850s – Italianate home – Archibald McEwen, a prosperous farmer and merchant, had a store on the same property.

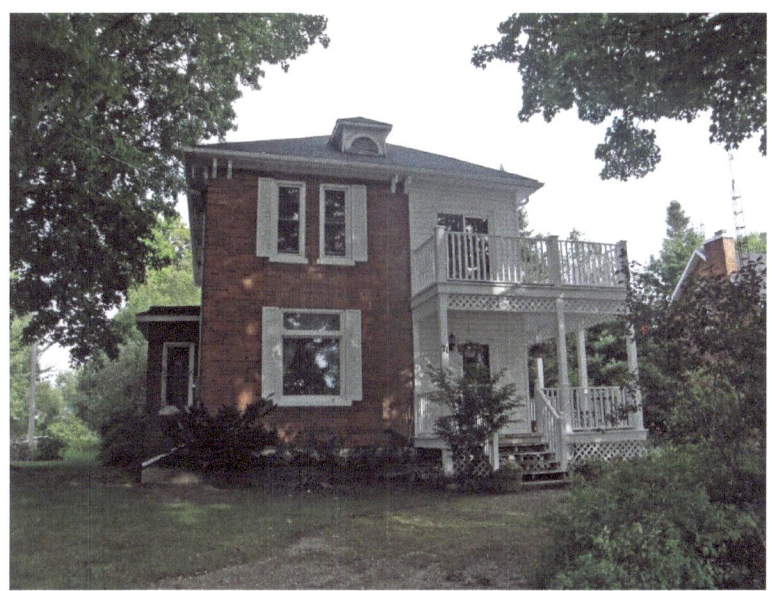

Neustadt - Italianate, hipped roof, second floor balcony

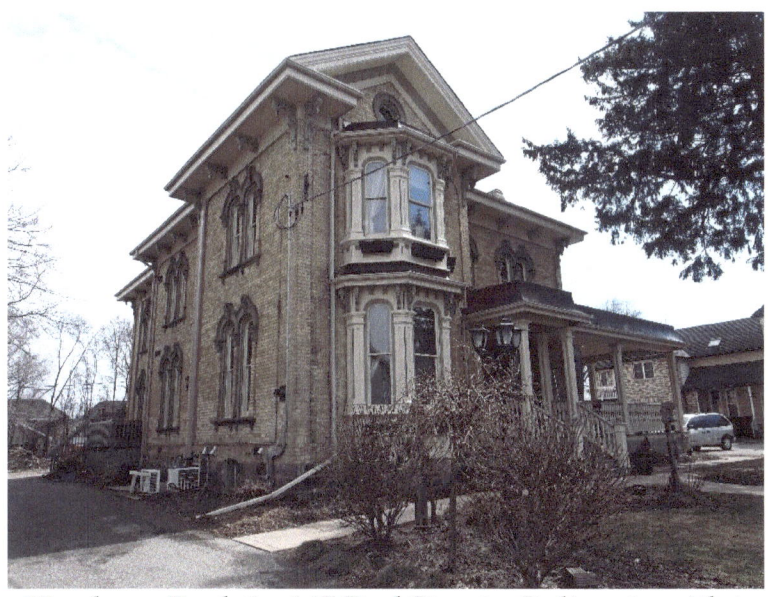

New Hamburg Book 1 - 145 Peel Street – Italianate with two-and-a-half storey tower-like bay, wraparound verandah, decorative window voussoirs and keystones, single cornice brackets

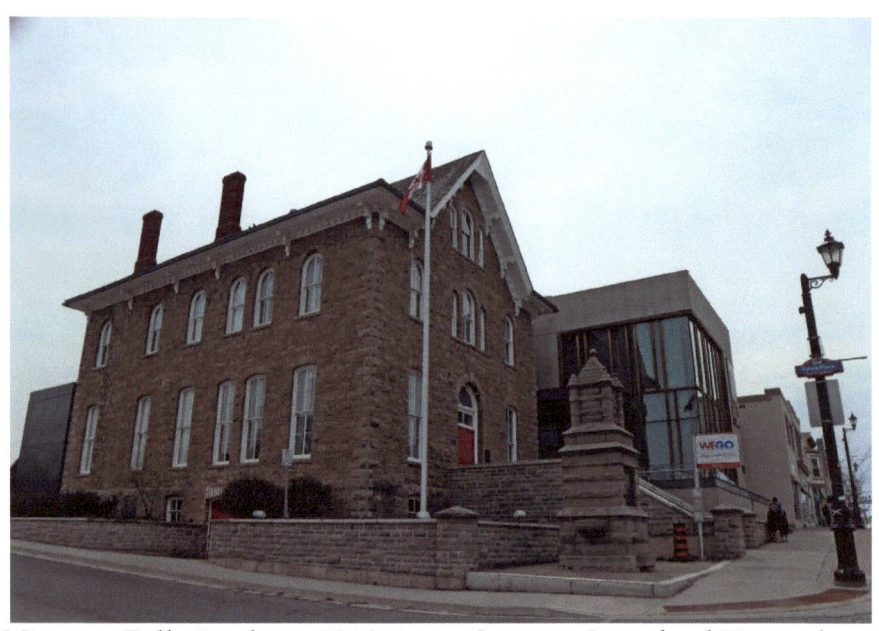

Niagara Falls Book 1 - 5810 Ferry Street – Stamford Township Hall was erected in 1874. It is now the Niagara Falls History Museum. The hall with its durable hammer dressed limestone construction in its eclectic Italianate styling includes a gabled hip roof with brackets and gingerbread trim, windows of different shape on the first and second storeys, and the main entrance archway with a keystone and voussoirs.

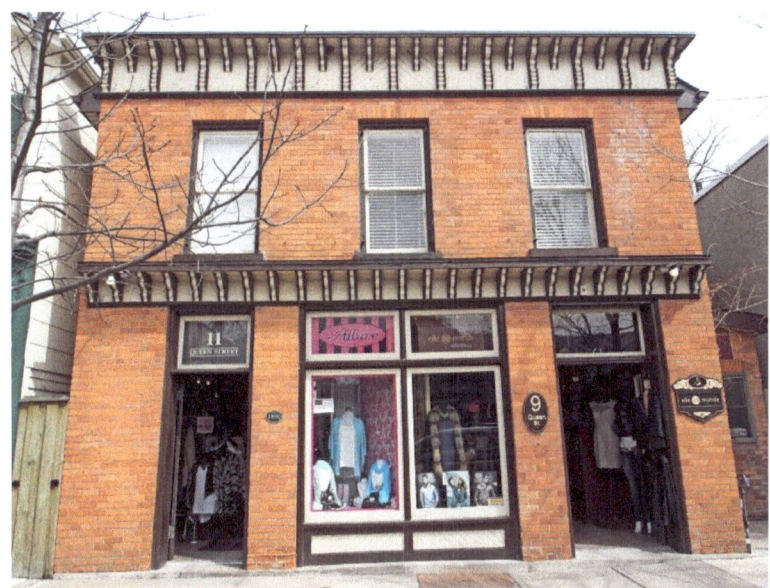

Niagara-on-the-Lake Book 1 - 9 and 11 Queen Street – c. 1890 – cornice brackets

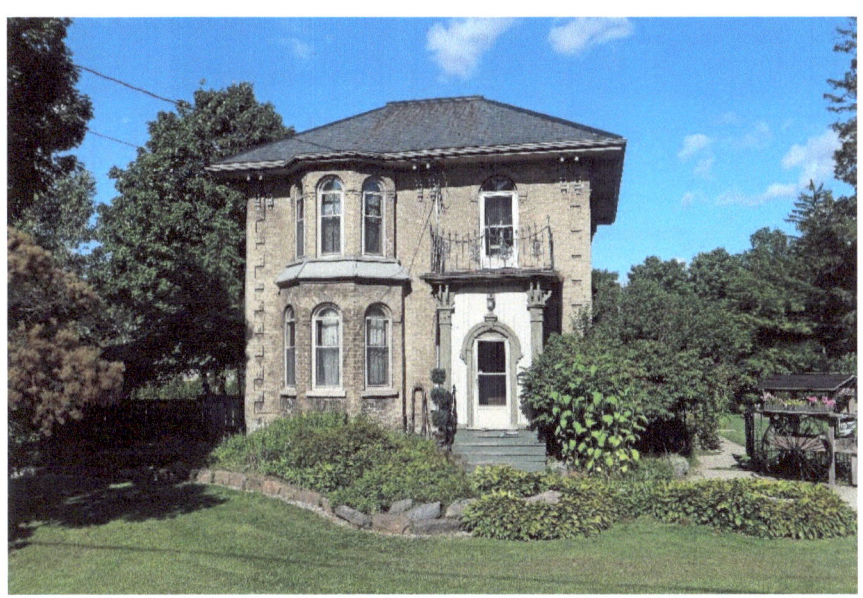

Norwich - Stover Street – Italianate, hipped roof, two-story bay window, balcony above enclosed front entrance, corner quoins

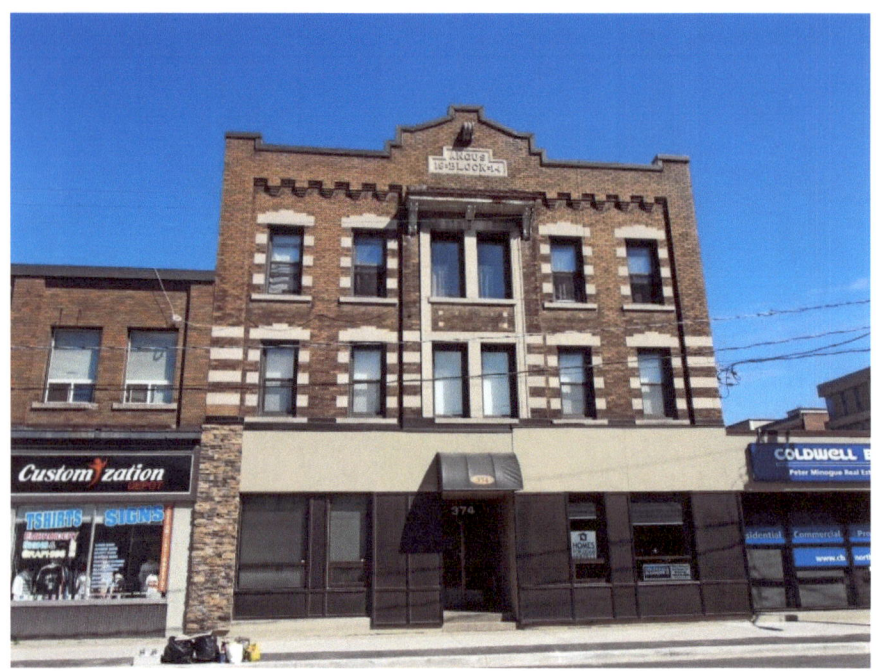

North Bay - 374 Fraser Street – Angus Block – 1914 – This building is noted for its parapet at the roof line and for its highly distinctive white stone window surrounds consisting of stepped lintels, quoined jambs and flat sills. Other notable features include the toothed heading of the in-stepped brick facing and bracketed canopy over the third-floor paired openings. The date stone indicates that H.W. Angus, an early architect in North Bay, was responsible for its design and erection.

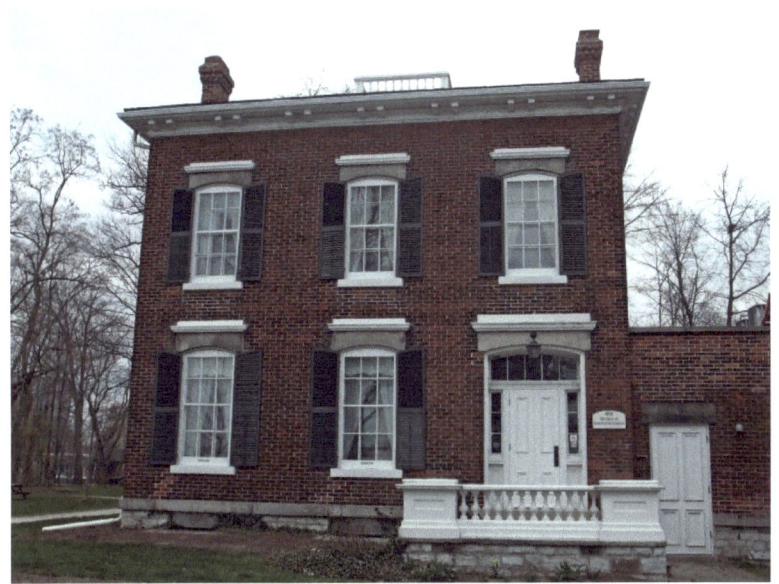

Oakville - Erchless built in 1858 by Robert Kerr Chisholm on the east bank of the harbour mouth

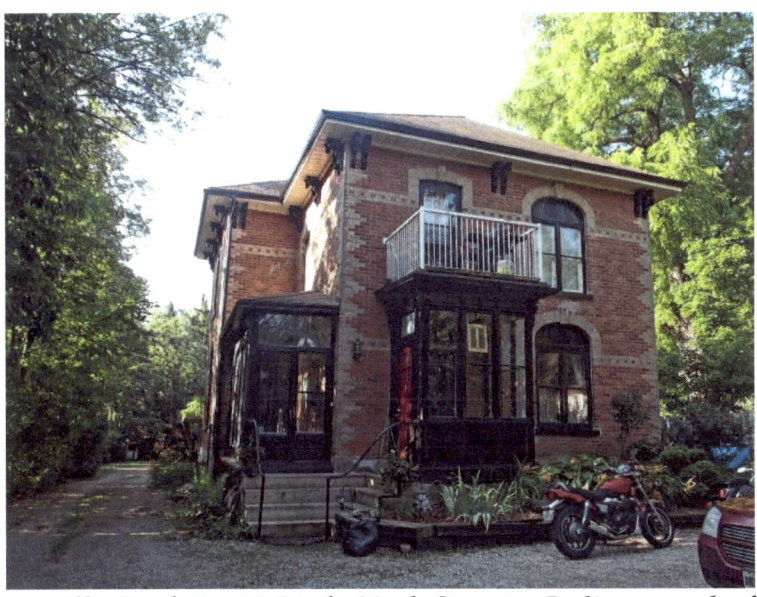

Orangeville Book 1 - 11 Little York Street – Italianate – buff-coloured brick banding and keystones and voussoirs, paired cornice brackets

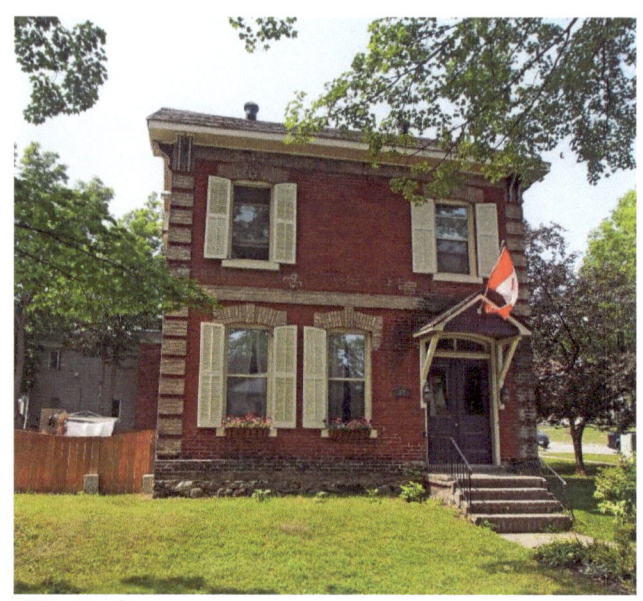

Orillia - #77 - Italianate – corner quoins

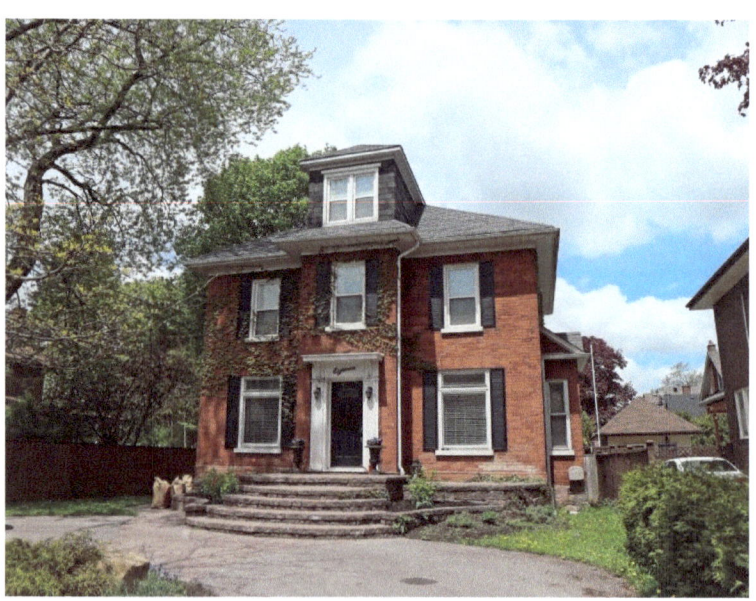

Oshawa Book 3 - 18 Aberdeen Street – two-story frontispiece, dormer

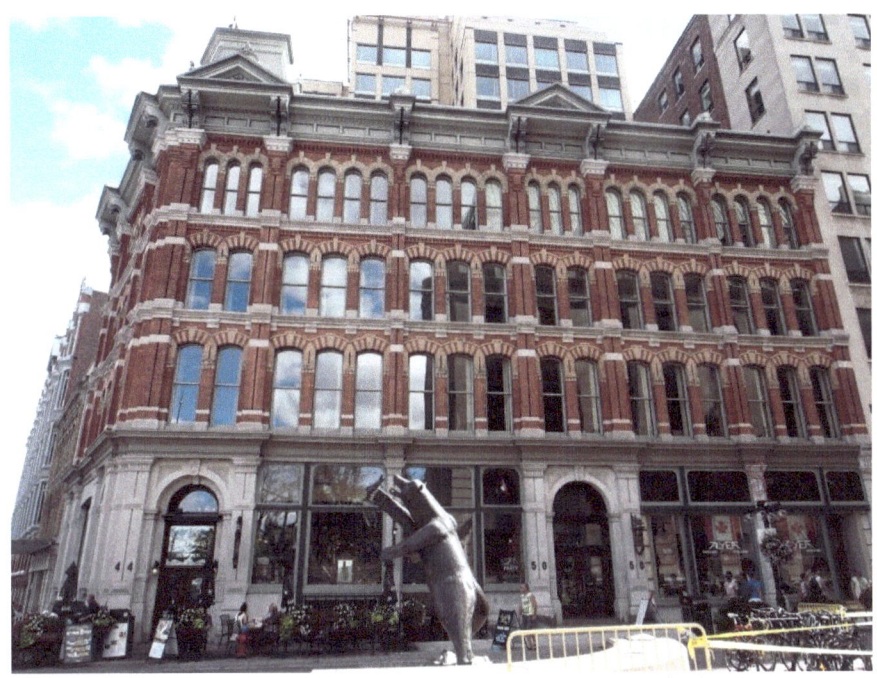

Ottawa Book 2 - 44-50 Sparks Street at corner of Elgin – Scottish Ontario Chambers – Italianate design - four-storey brick building with a high ground floor, balanced façade, decorative multi-coloured masonry, radiated voussoirs of multicolored brick, fenestration (the arrangement, design and proportioning of windows and doors), roof line with heavy bracketing and decorated cornice

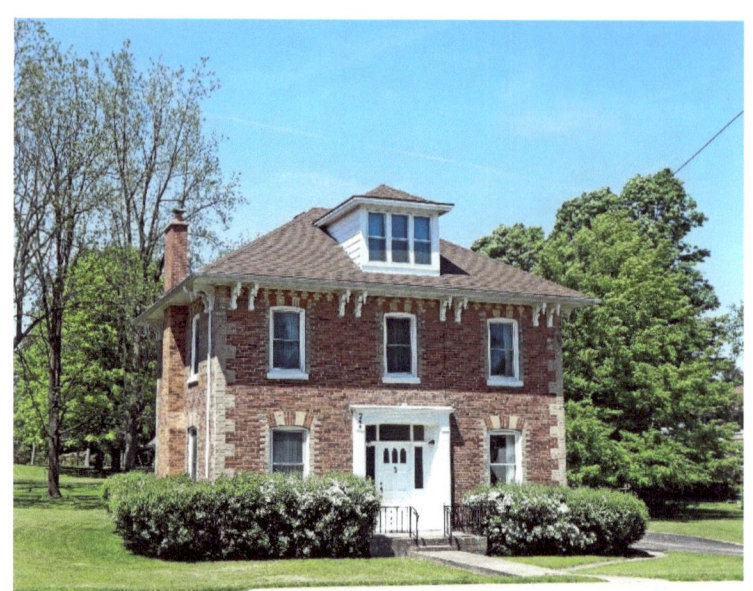

Otterville - 244 Main Street East – dormer in attic, paired cornice brackets, corner quoins, dichromatic voussoirs

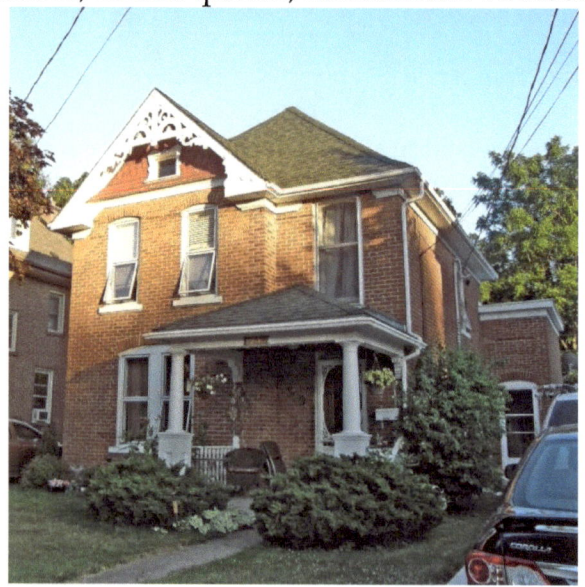

Owen Sound Book 1 - #359 – fancy gingerbread trim – Italianate with 2½ storey frontispiece, verge board trim on gable

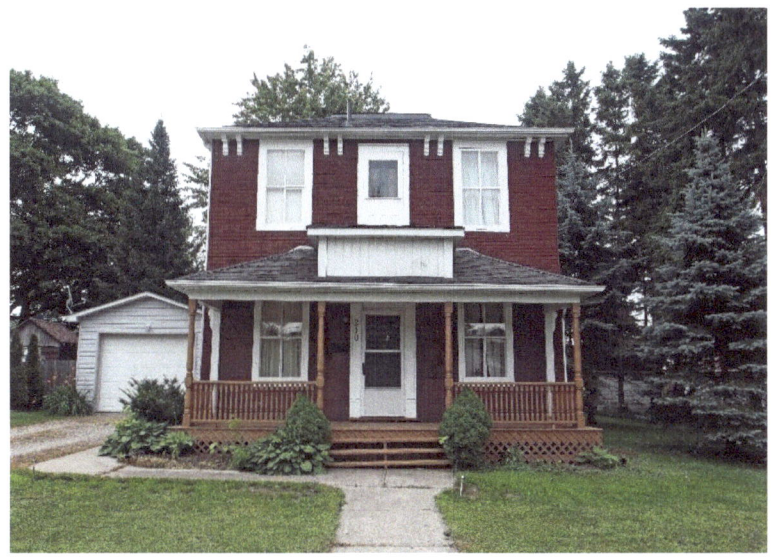

Palmerston - 210 Queen Street – Italianate, cornice brackets

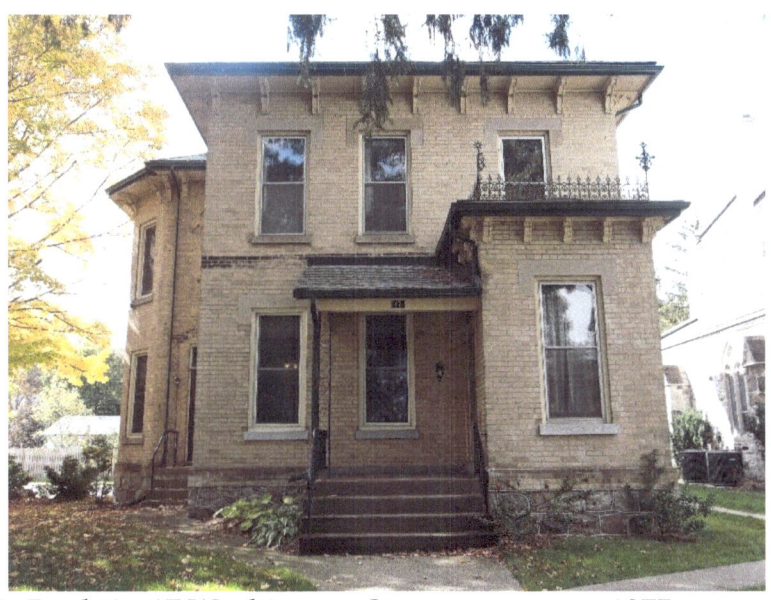

Paris Book 1 - 17 Washington Street – rectory – 1875 - Italianate style, yellow brick, iron cresting above square bay window, single cornice brackets

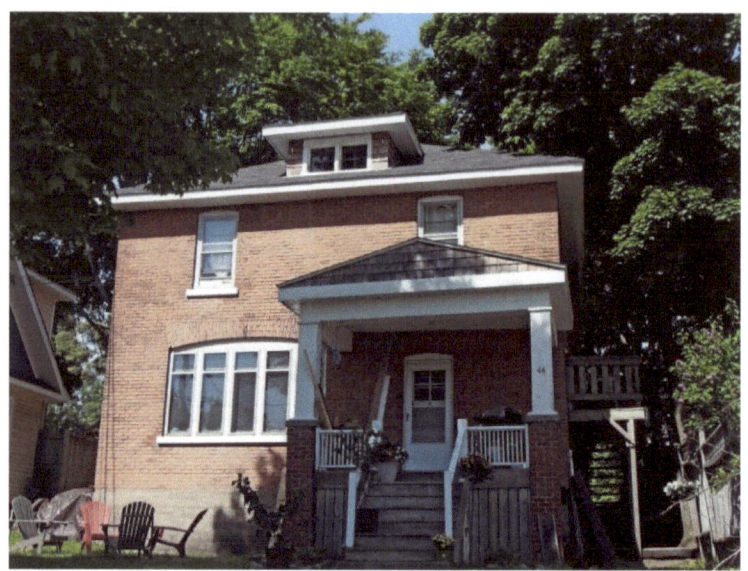

Parry Sound - 44 Church Street – Italianate – hipped roof with dormer

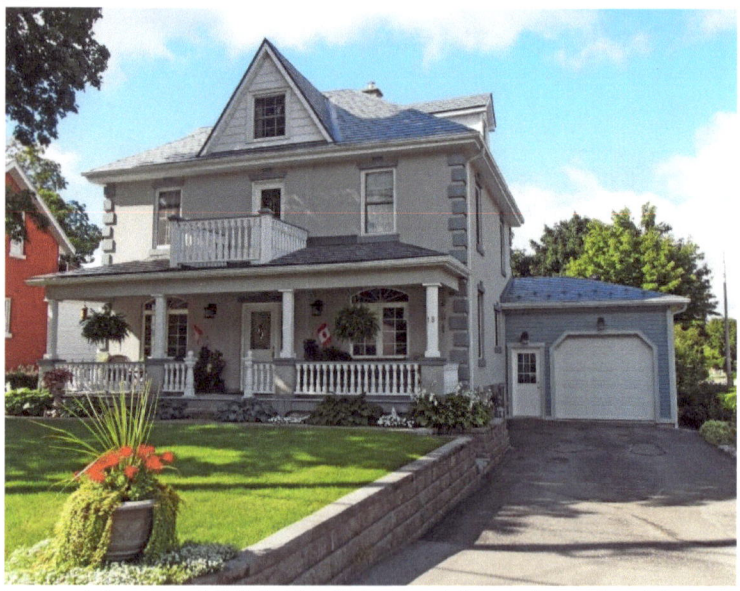

Penetanguishene - 18 Maria Street – hipped roof with dormers, second floor balcony, corner quoins, multi-paned transom windows above large first storey windows, open spindle railing

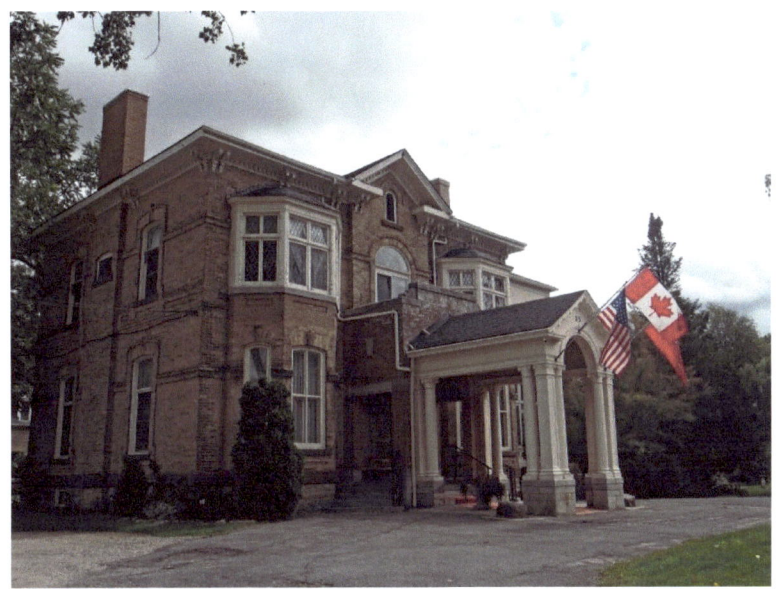

Perth - 23 Drummond Street West – Italianate – two-storey bay windows, paired cornice brackets, banding, composite entrance pillars

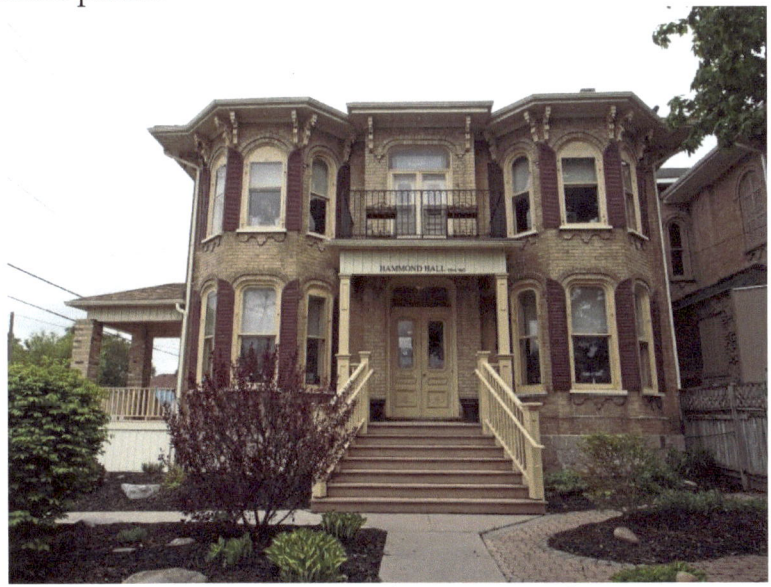

Peterborough Book 2 - 232 Brock Street – Italianate, cornice brackets, two-storey bay windows, second floor balcony

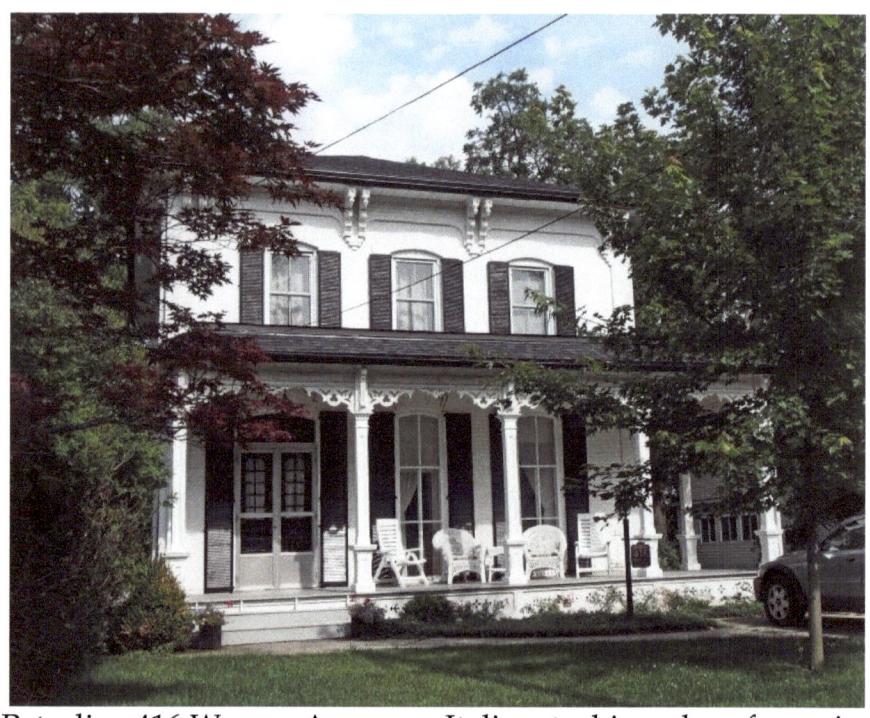

Petrolia - 416 Warren Avenue – Italianate, hipped roof, cornice brackets, bric-a-brac on verandah

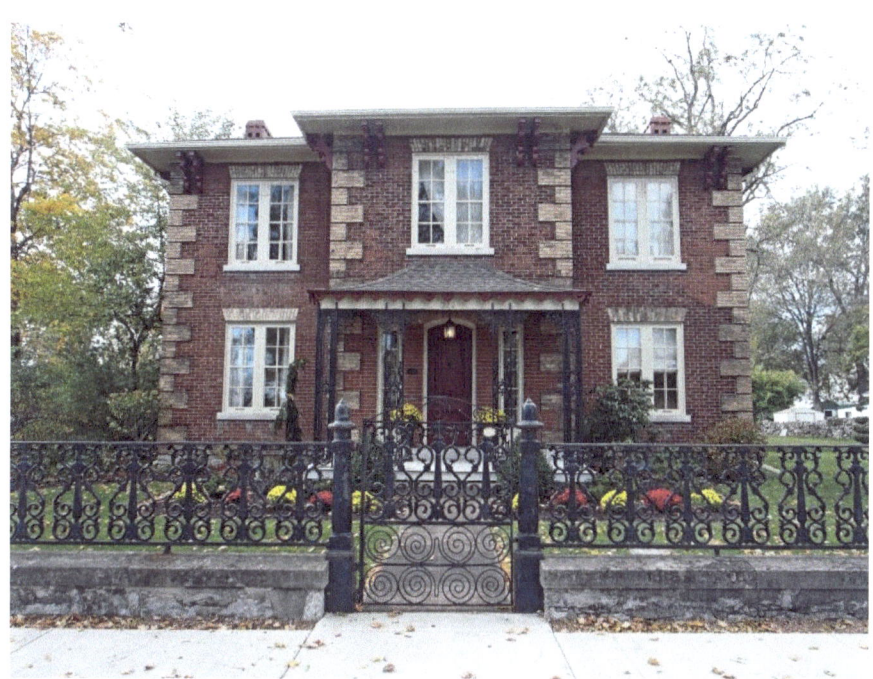

Port Colborne Book 1 - 322 King Street – Ingleside – It was built in 1867 for Charles H. Carter and occupied by the Carter family for 118 years, including Port Colborne's first mayor, Dewitt Carter. The two-storey structure has projecting eaves supported by paired cornice brackets and corner quoins in dichromatic brick characteristic of Italianate architecture. Its rectangular plan with projecting frontispiece and hipped roof indicate it is a version of a house plan popularized by the magazine "The Canada Farmer" in 1865. The grounds are surrounded by a locally produced cast iron fence.

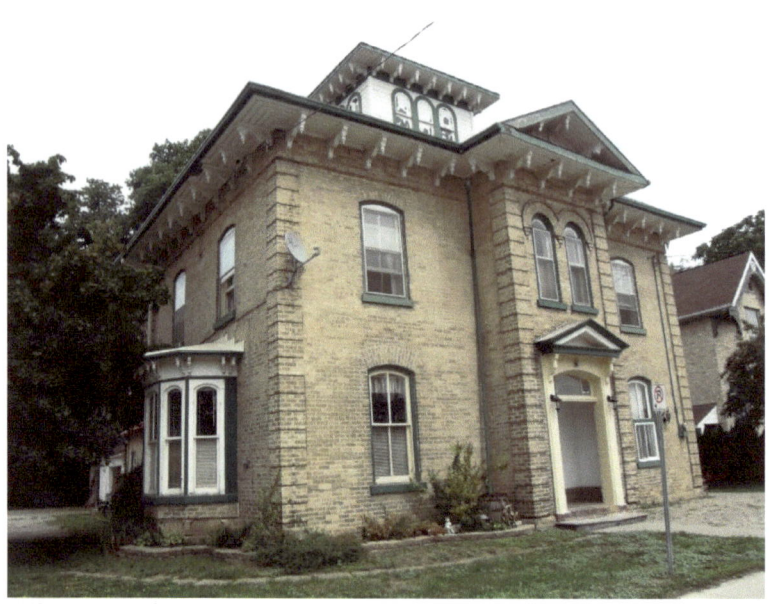

Port Elgin Book 1 - Italianate with belvedere on roof, two storey frontispiece with triangular pediment and arched window hoods, single cornice brackets, bay window on side

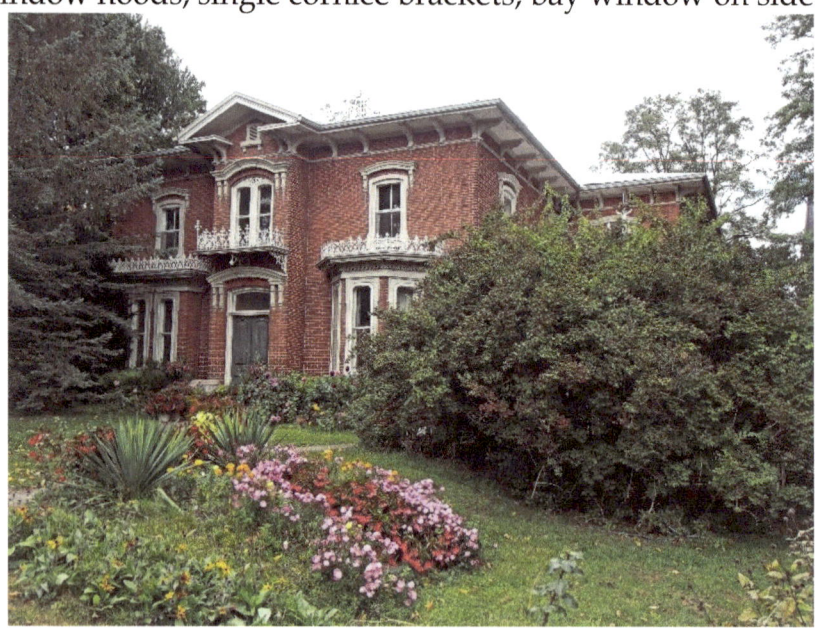

Port Hope Book 1 - Walton Street – Italianate style – iron cresting above bay windows and entrance, cornice brackets

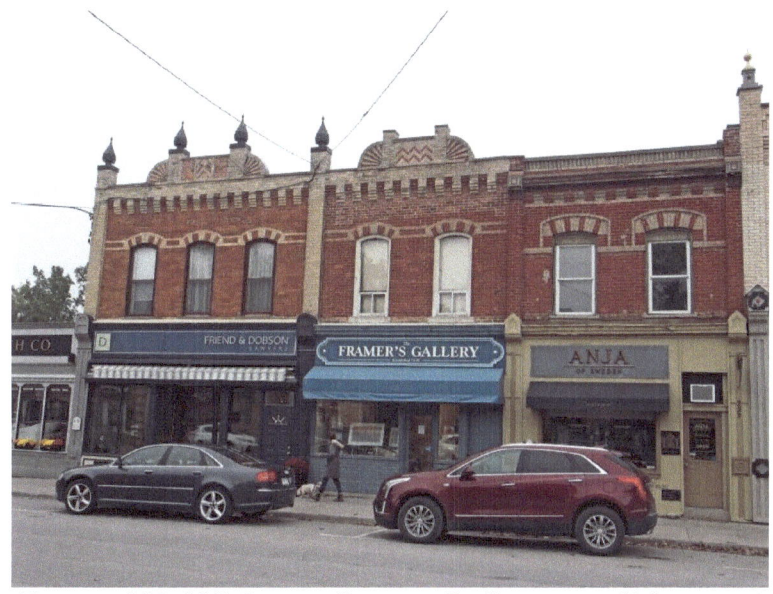

Port Perry - 229-235 Queen Street – Italianate – dichromatic brickwork, banding, finials

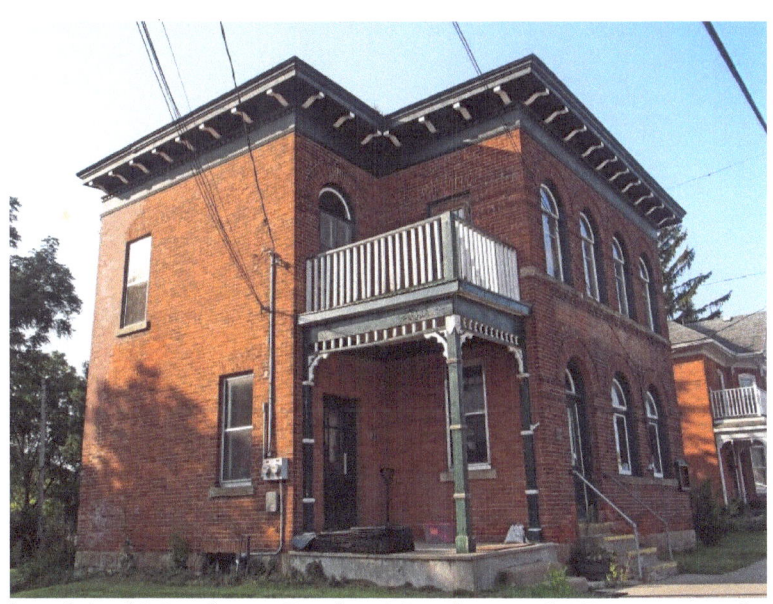

Portland and Newboro Book – Newboro - 24 Drummond Street – Italianate – Union Bank Building – cornice brackets, second floor balcony, voussoirs, string course

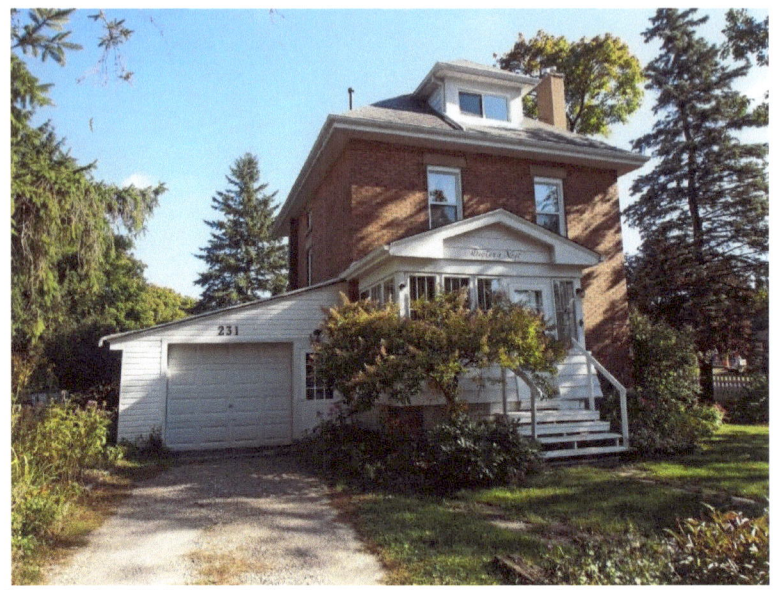

Rockwood - 231 Guelph Street – Italianate, hipped roof, dormer

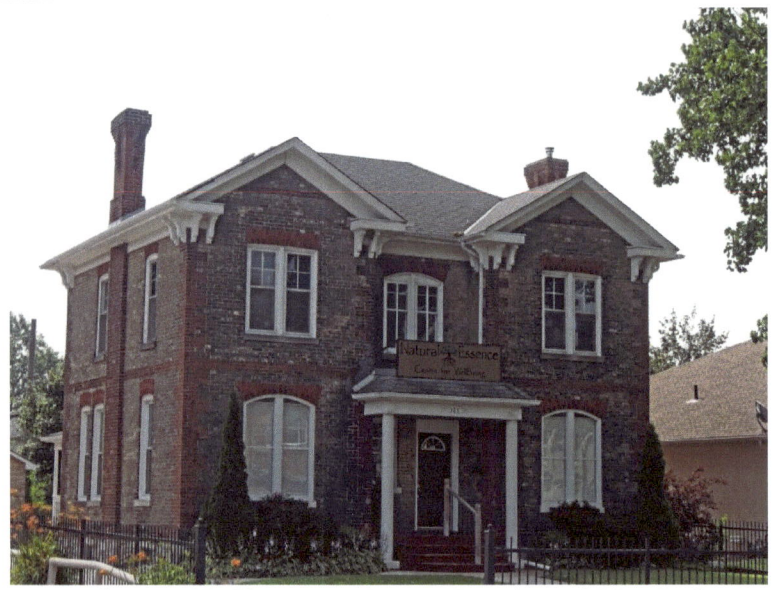

Sarnia Book 1 - 168 Christina Street South – 1890 – Italianate, cornice brackets, dichromatic brickwork, banding

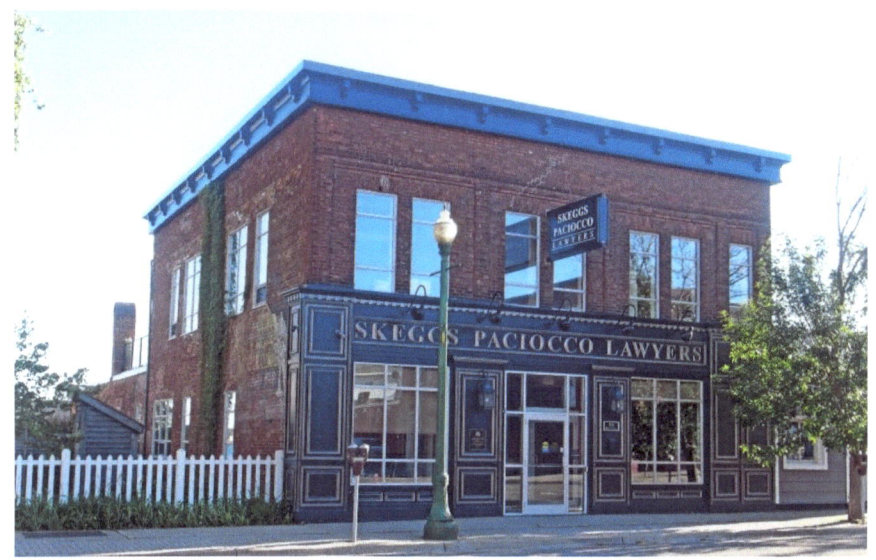

Sault Ste. Marie - 819 Queen Street East – cornice brackets

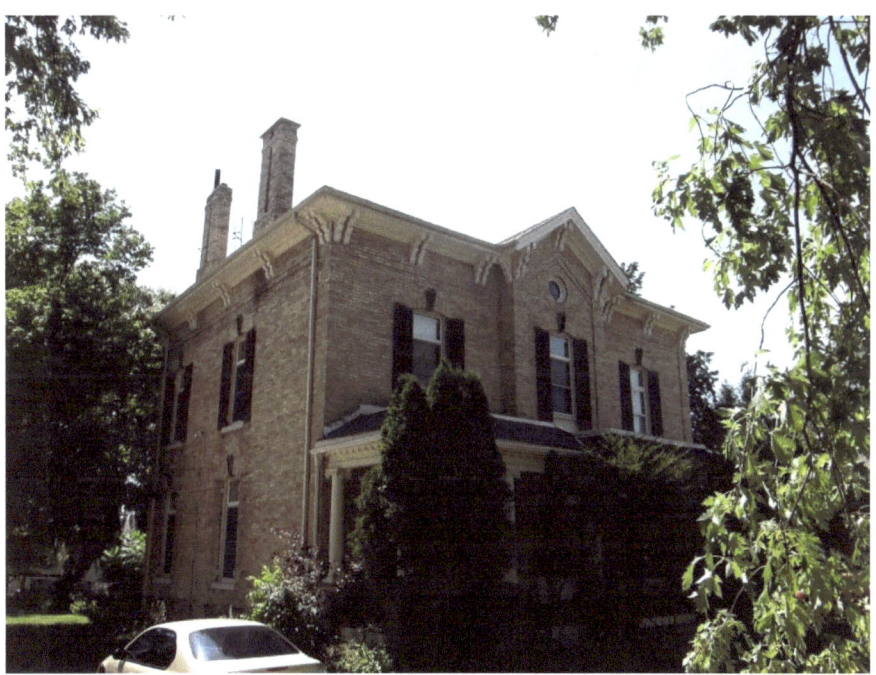

Seaforth - Italianate – cornice brackets

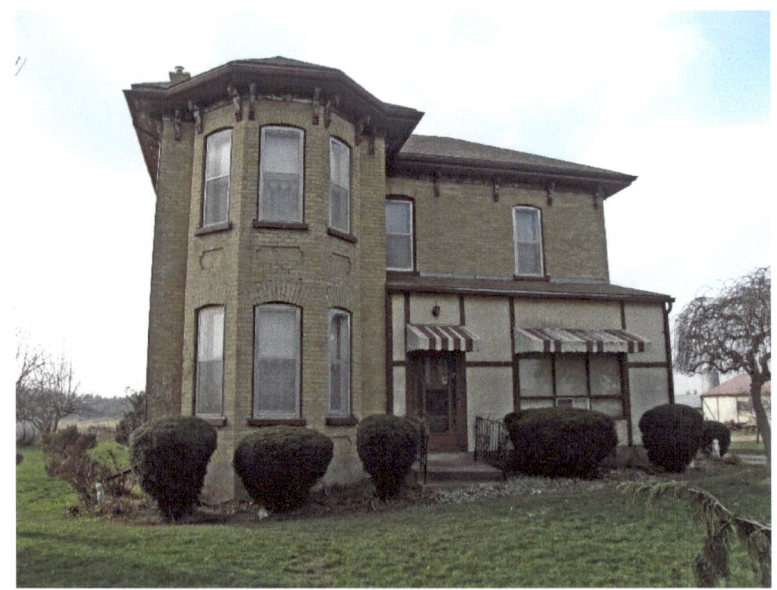

Sheffield – Italianate – cornice brackets, two-story bay window

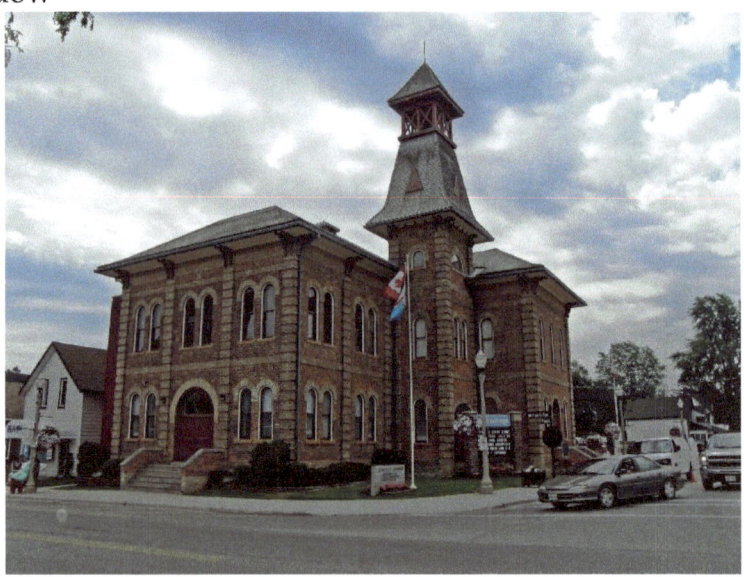

Shelburne Administration, Grace Tipling Hall, Police Station - corner of Main Street East and Victoria Street – Italianate style, paired cornice brackets, dichromatic brickwork, three-storey tower with cap and cupola

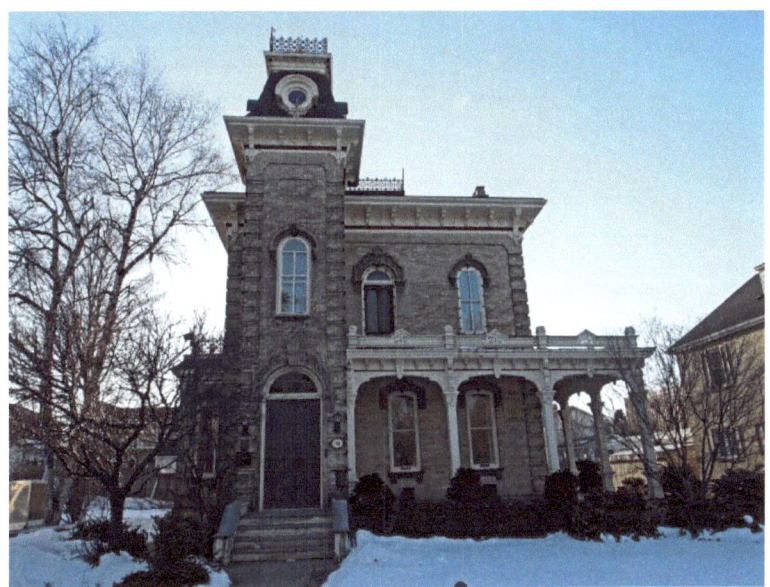

Simcoe - 94 Norfolk Street – Italianate style with two-and-a-half storey tower-like bay topped with a cupola with iron cresting on top; decorative voussoirs and keystones

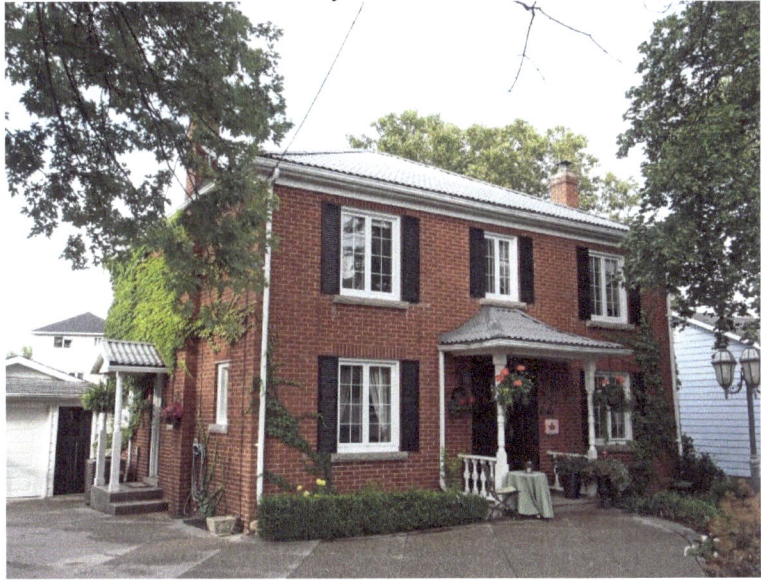

Smithville - 157 West Street – hipped roof, balanced façade, shutters

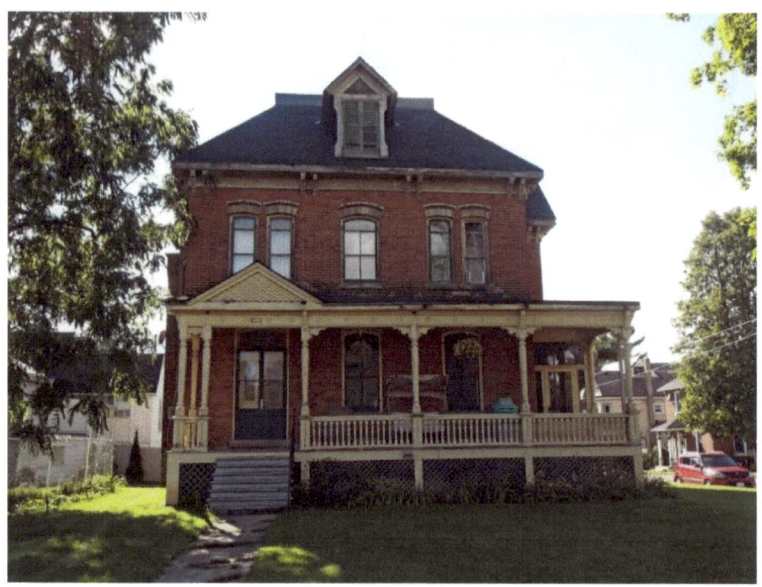

Smiths Falls - 102 Brockville Street – Italianate - steeply pitched hip roof with dormer; cornice brackets, voussoirs; turned veranda roof supports with decorative capitals, open railing; pediment

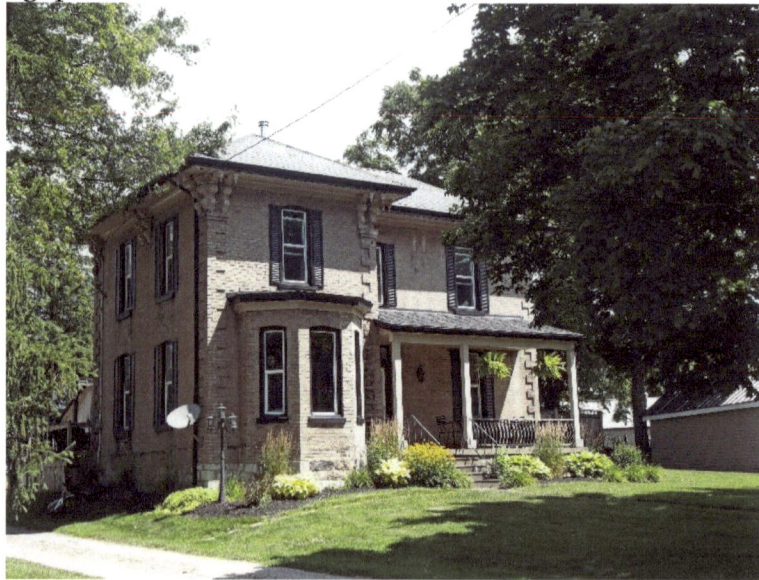

Southwest Oxford Township – Salford - Dereham Line – Italianate – cornice brackets, corner quoins, bay window

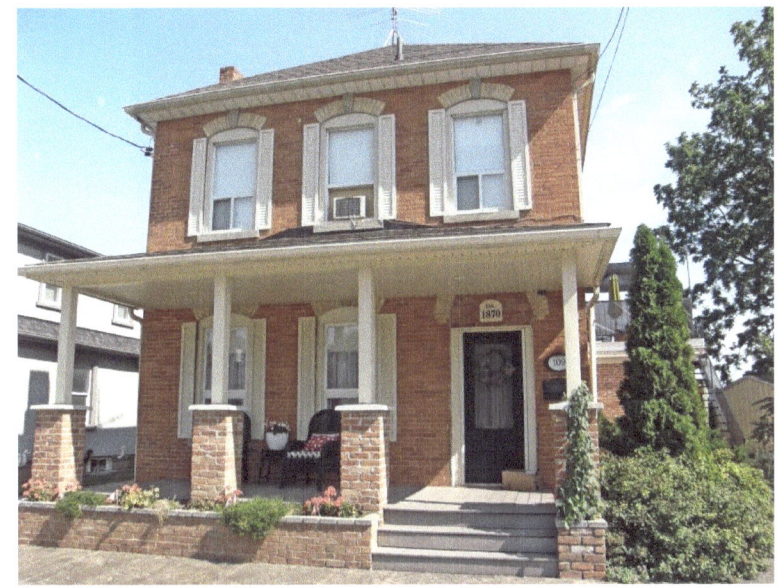

St. Catharines - 109 Main Street – two storey, Italianate, hipped roof, keystones and voussoirs above windows and door

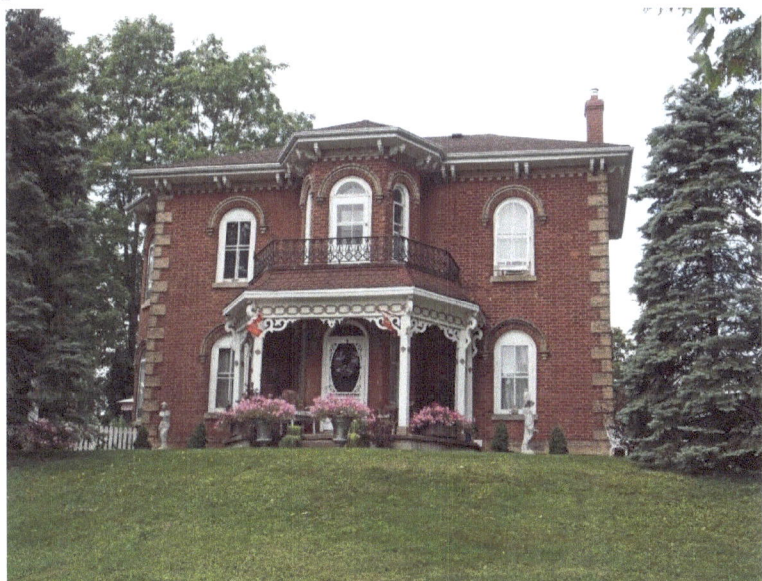

St. George - 6 Thompson Street – Two Roses Bed & Breakfast – Italianate – bay window with balcony, corner quoins

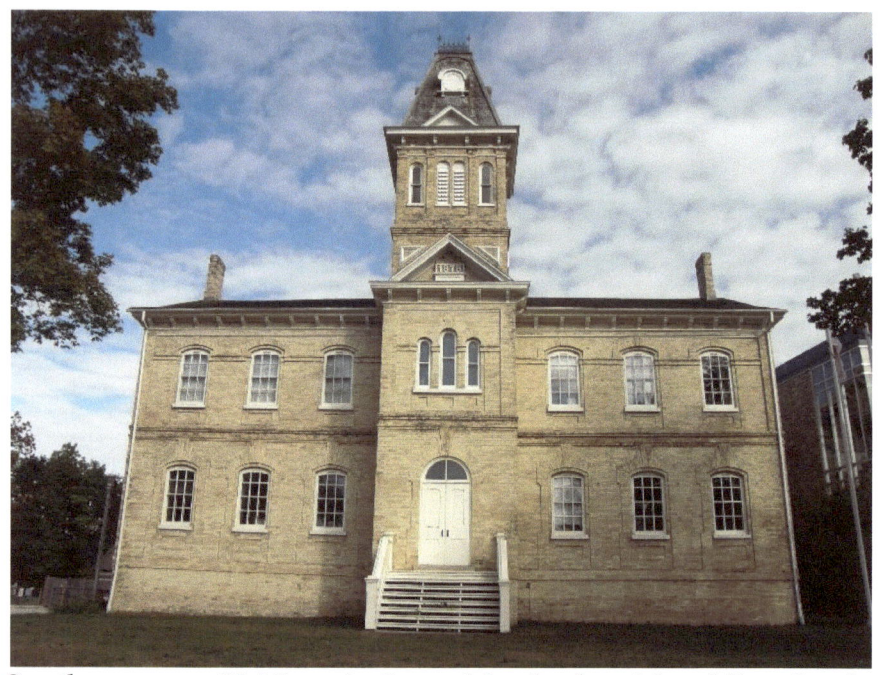

Southampton - 33 Victoria Street North, the old public school – now houses the Bruce County Museum and Cultural Centre - 1878 – yellow brick – Italianate style with two-and-a-half storey tower-like bay with two-storey tower above, iron cresting on top

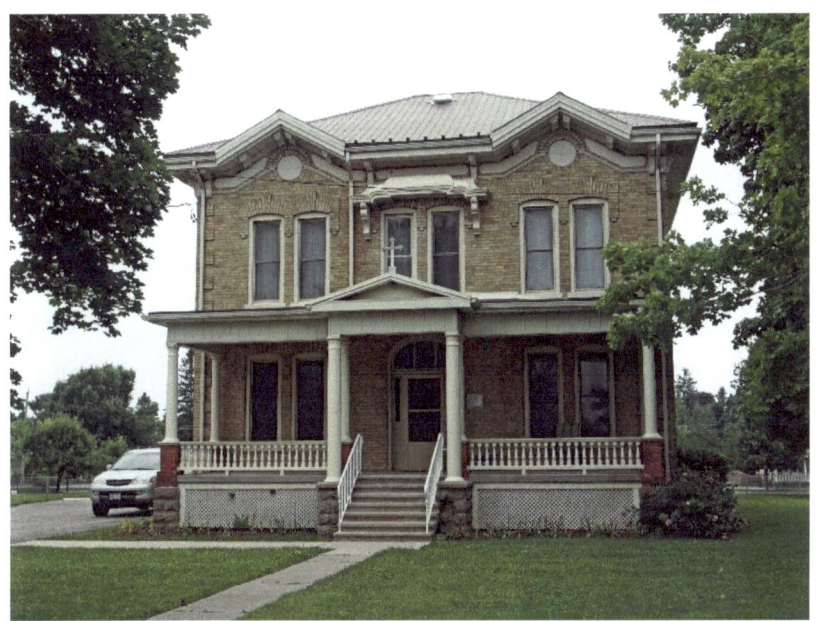

St. Jacobs Book - St. Clements - Lobsinger Line – Italianate, hipped roof, pediment

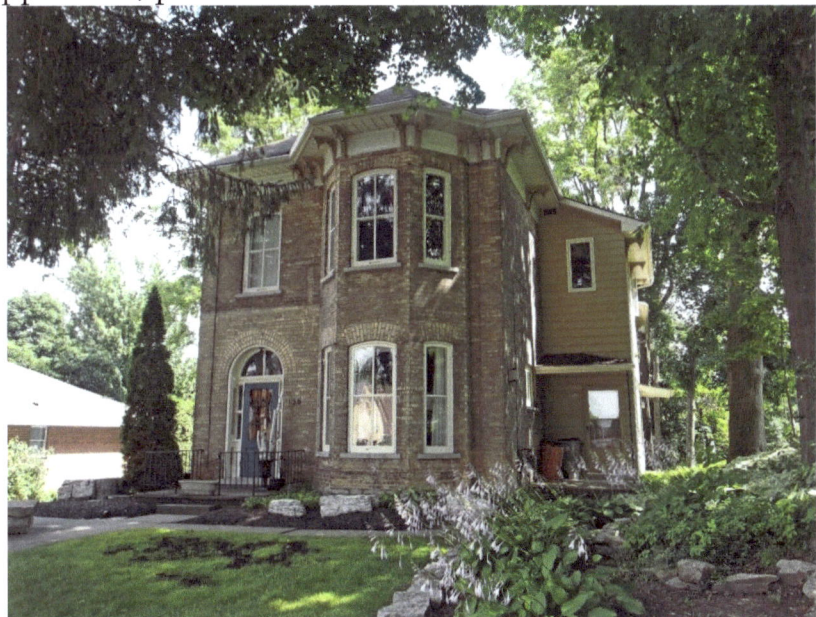

St. Marys Book 2 - 136 Queen Street West – Italianate – cornice brackets, two-storey tower-like bay

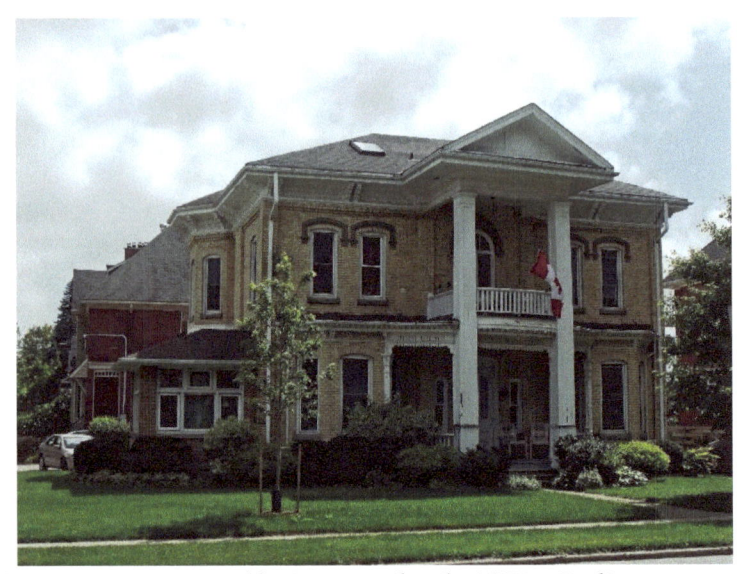

St. Thomas - 91 Metcalfe Street – built 1871 - Italianate – single cornice brackets, pediment above second floor balcony, arched voussoirs, Greek Revival porch supported by Ionic columns

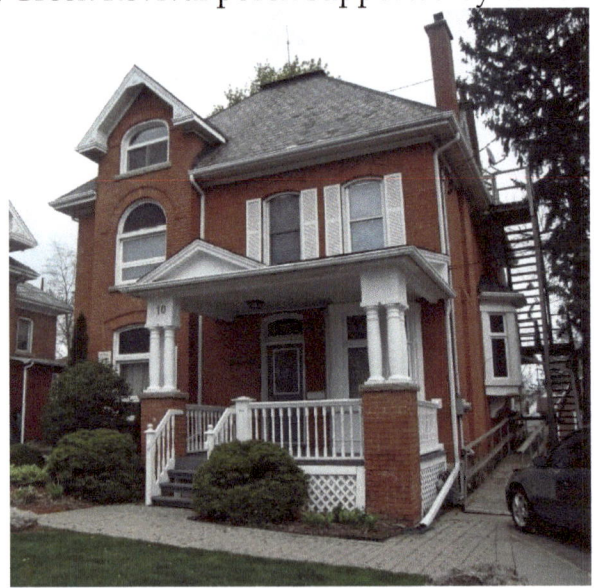

Stoney Creek - 10 Lake Avenue – Italianate with two-and-a-half storey tower-like bay with cornice return on gable, pediment above verandah

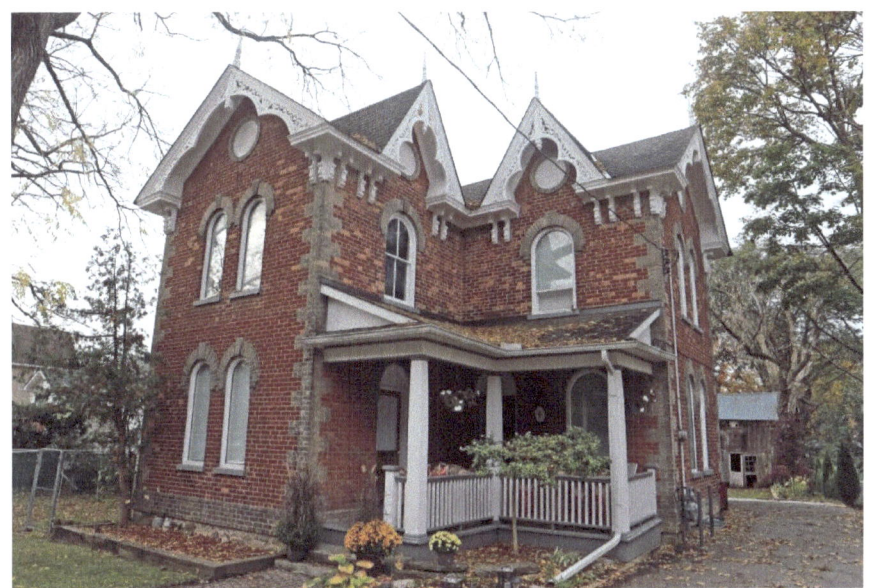

Stouffville Book 1 - 6 Albert Street – Built in 1878 for Jacob Raymer, a miller – Late Victorian hybrid with Italianate features

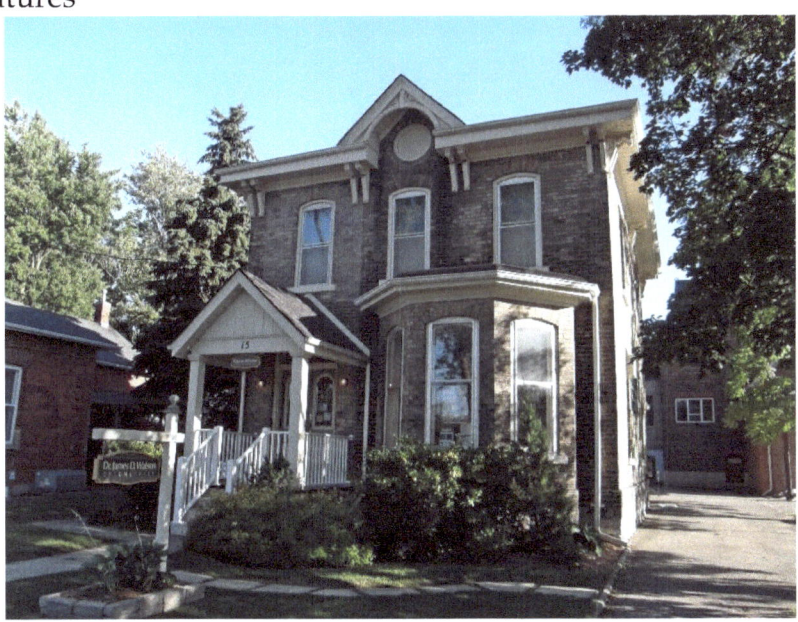

Stratford - 15 Grange Street – Italianate, paired cornice brackets, ground-floor bay window

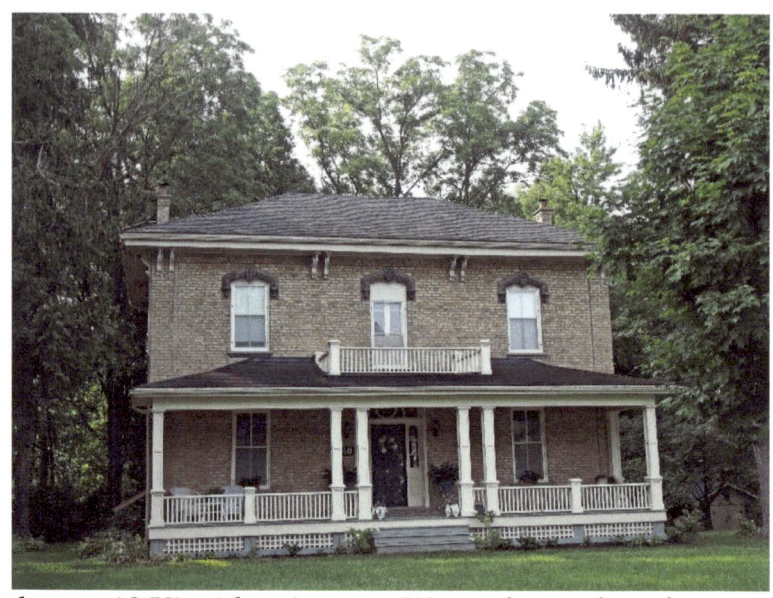

Strathroy - 10 Kittridge Avenue West – hipped roof, paired cornice brackets, center balcony above full-width veranda

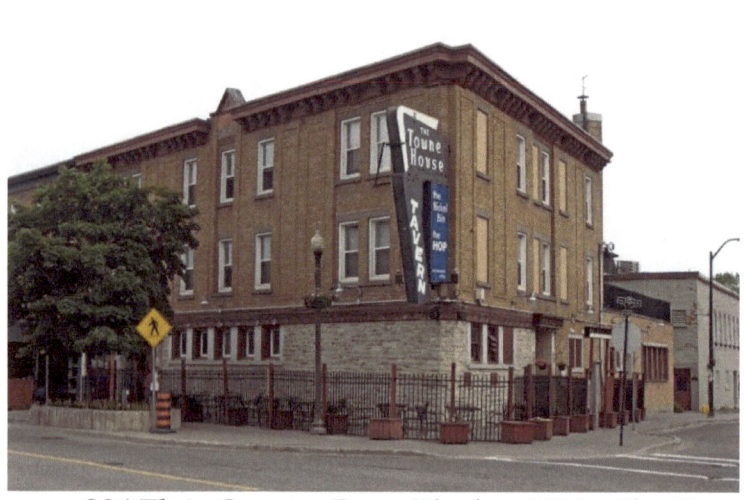

Sudbury - 206 Elgin Street – Prete Block – 1914 - The Towne House Tavern

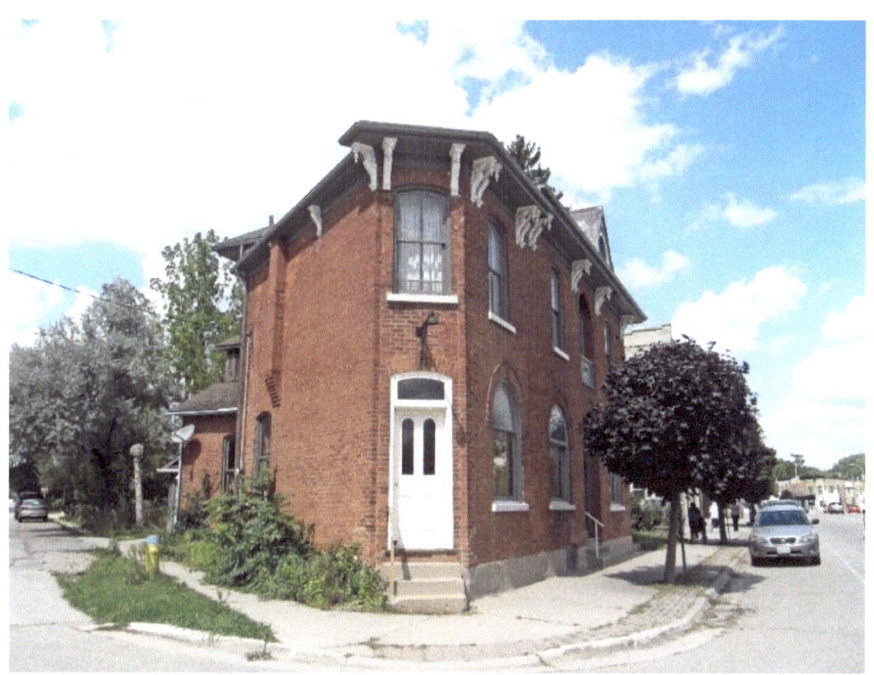

Tavistock - 52 Woodstock Street South - The Glass Swan – This late Italianate style has existed since 1892 when Dr. Otto Niemeier bricked over two adjoining structures; it is one of the oldest remaining in Tavistock and was the location of several early merchants and doctors.

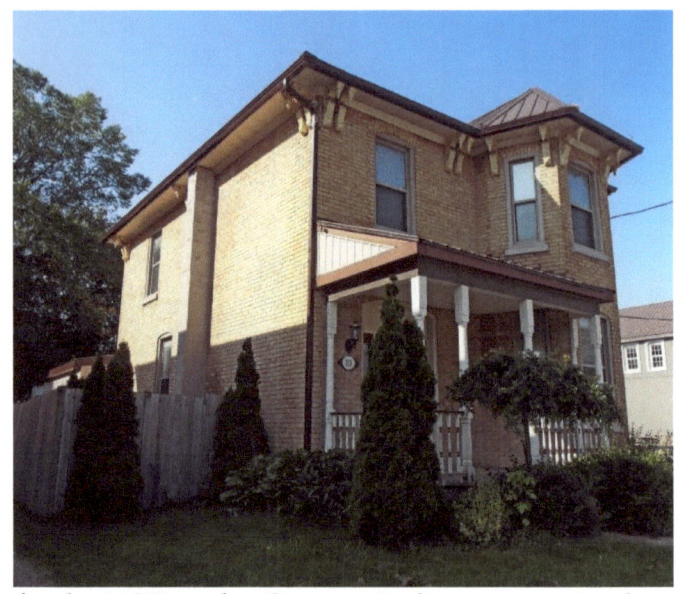

Thamesford - 113 Dundas Street – Italianate – paired cornice brackets, wood-turned verandah supports

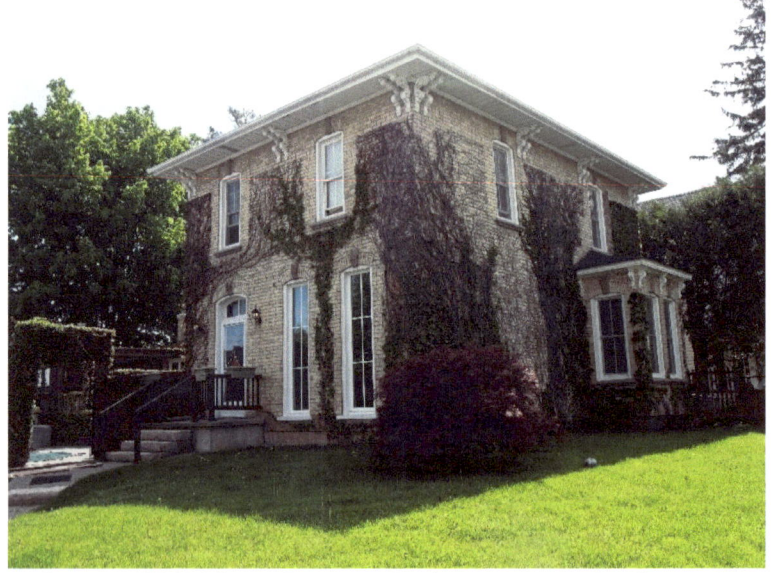

Tillsonburg - 59 Ridout Street – Italianate – paired cornice brackets, bay window, voussoirs and keystones, transom window

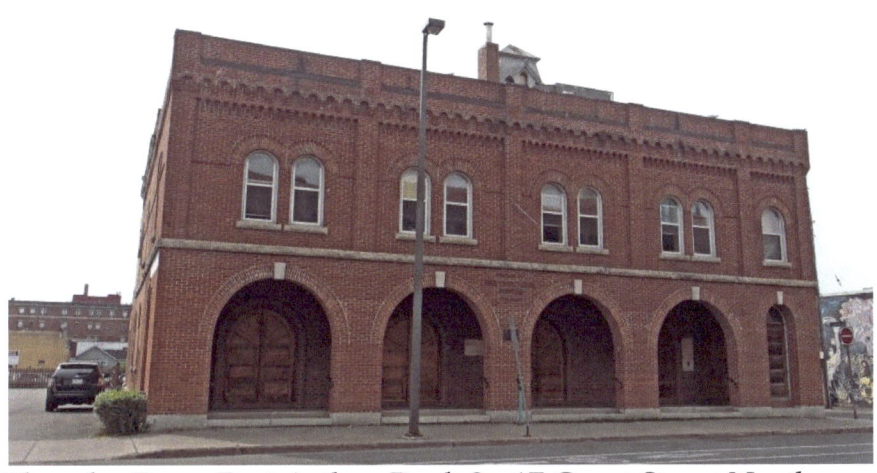

Thunder Bay – Port Arthur Book 2 - 17 Court Street North – formerly the central Fire Station and now the Multicultural Association – The fire hall was constructed in 1906 in the Italianate style. It has corbelled brickwork, arched windows connected by brick stringcourses, and a hose-drying tower. The brick two-storey structure was designed for horse-drawn fire wagons with access provided by four round arched wooden doors. Shallow brick pilasters divide the façade into four-and-a-half bays, four for the wagon doors and the half for an ordinary round-arched doorway. On the second storey are paired arched windows, and horizontal rows of ornamental brick work with a simple parapet at the roofline.

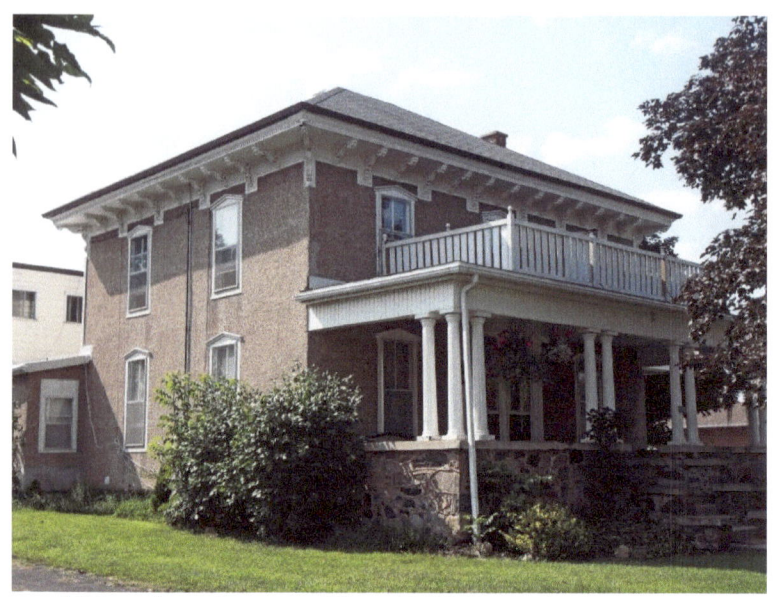

Town of Lincoln – Beamsville - 4382 Ontario Street – cornice brackets, second floor balcony

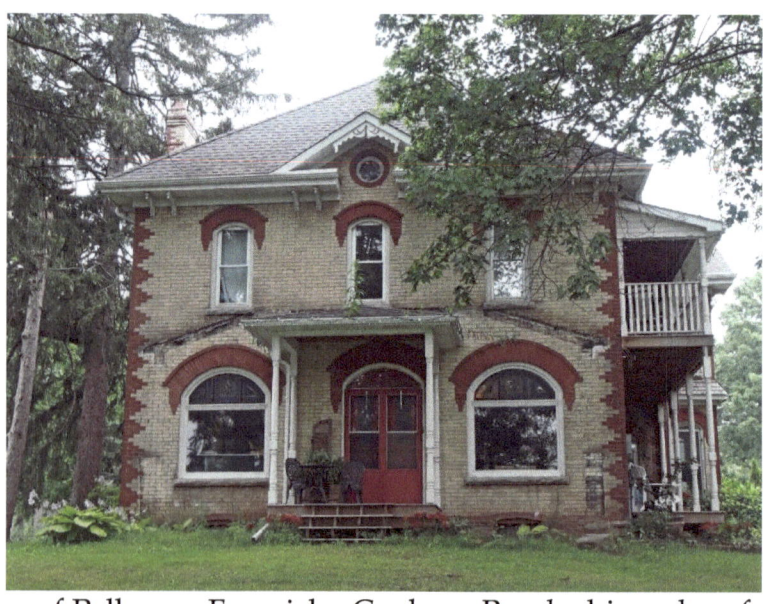

Town of Pelham – Fenwick - Canboro Road – hipped roof, corner quoins, voussoirs

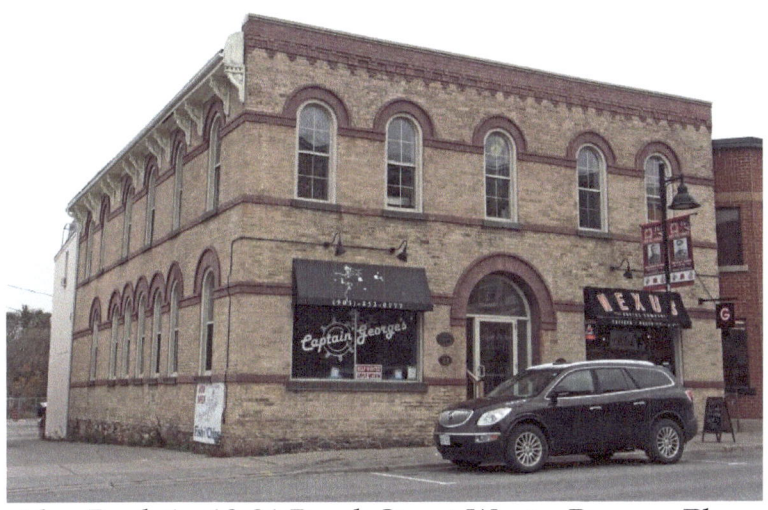

Uxbridge Book 1 - 19-21 Brock Street West – Bascom Place Hotel – now Captain George's Fish 'n' Chips – paired cornice brackets, dentil molding, voussoirs connected with banding

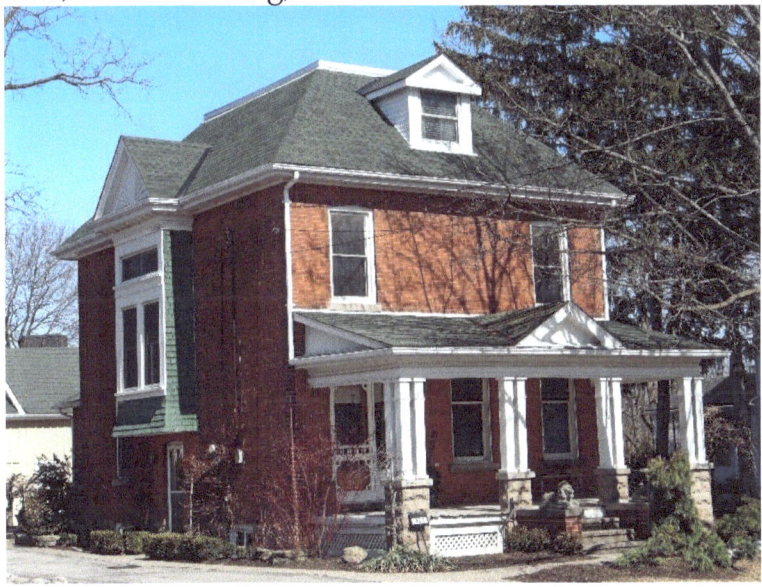

Waterdown - 122 Mill Street – Italianate with dormer in attic, pediment above verandah

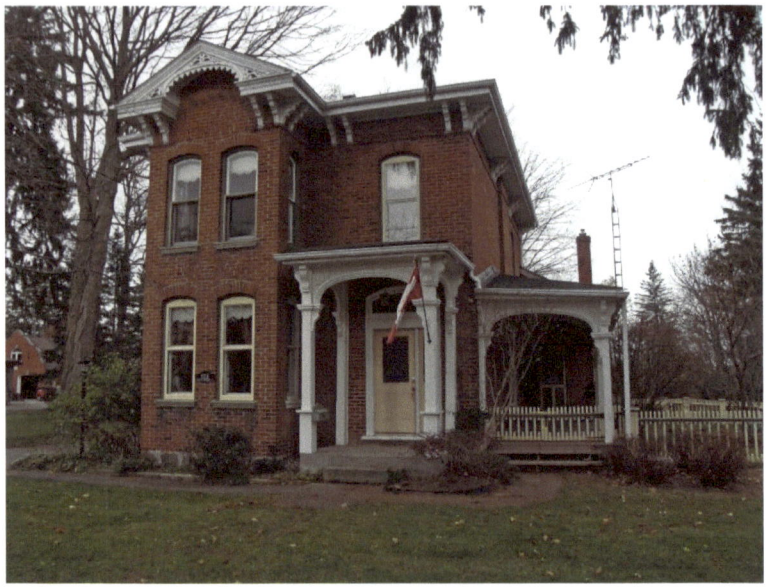

Waterford - 173 Main Street – two-storey tower-like bay capped with bargeboard trim on gable

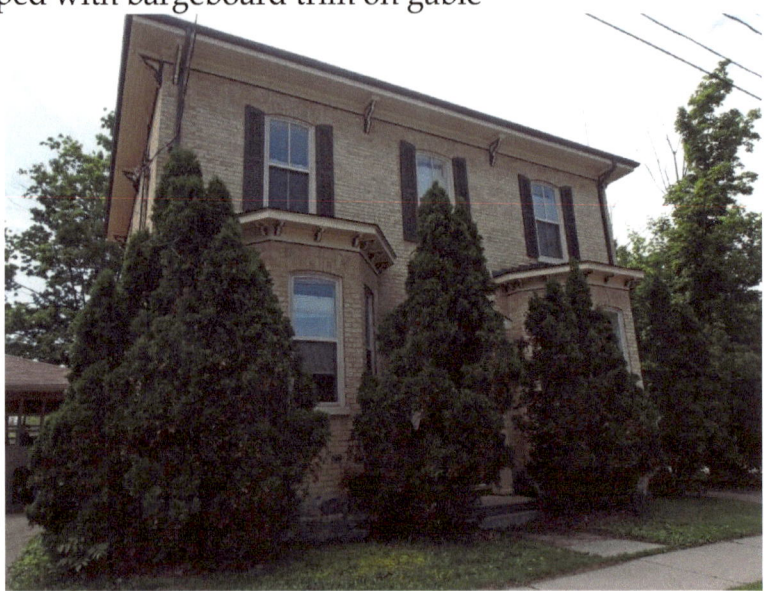

Waterloo Book 1 - 119 Albert Street – Italianate in buff brick, single cornice brackets, bay windows

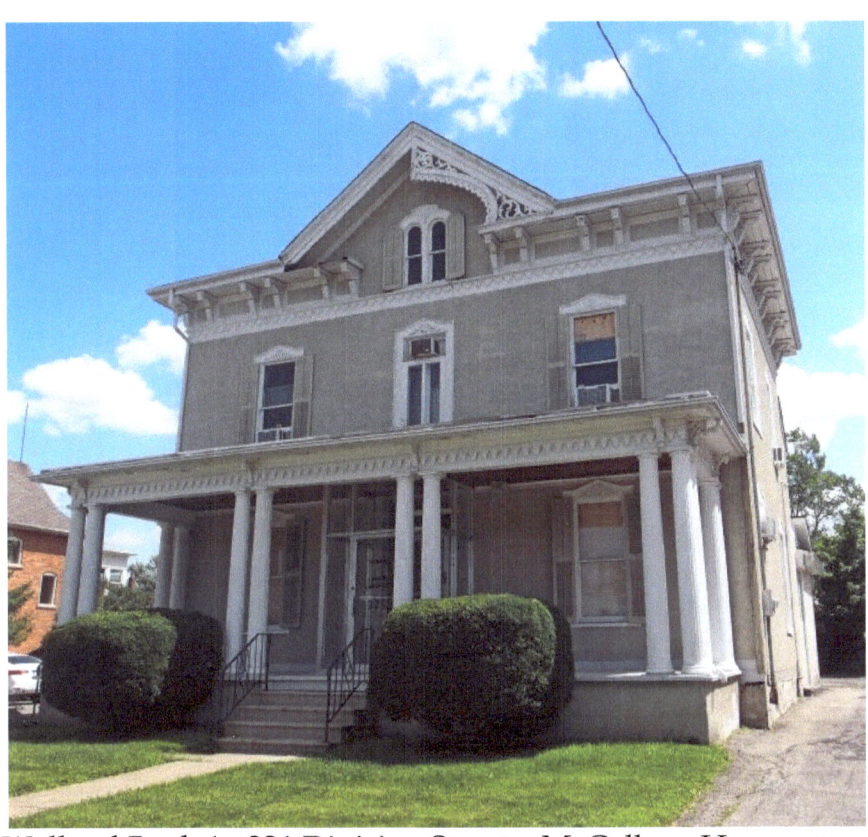

Welland Book 1 - 221 Division Street – McCollum-Harcourt House – late 1870s - 2½ storey stuccoed house, Italianate style – open verandah supported by wooden columns, double eave brackets, lacy verge board under central peak above a double semi-circular window

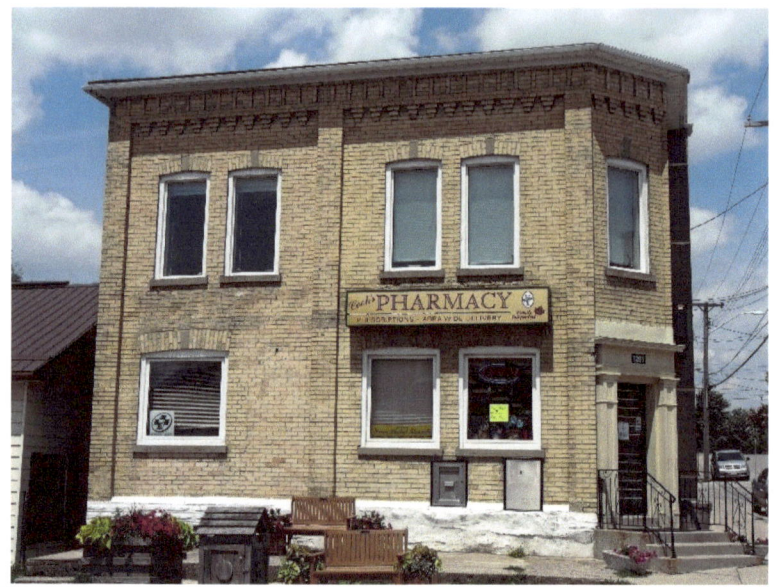

Wellesley - 1201 Queen's Bush Road – Italianate, dentil moulding

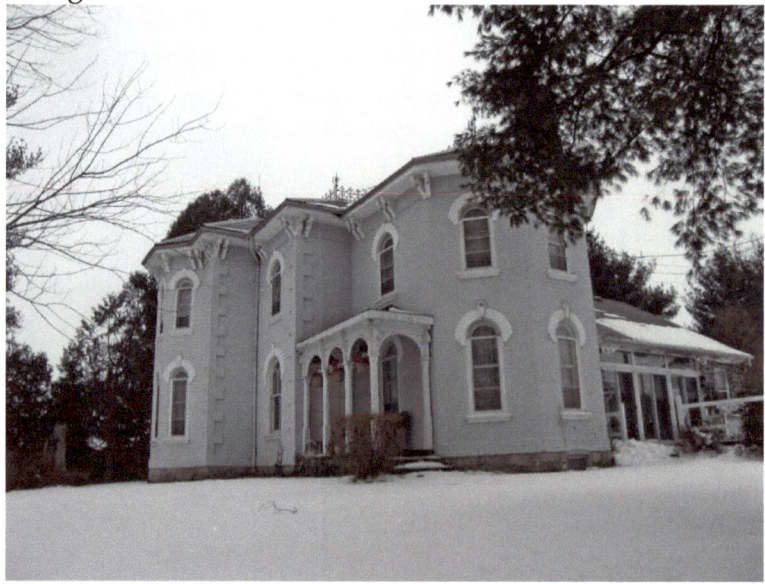

West Flamborough – Concession 2 - cornice brackets, corner quoins

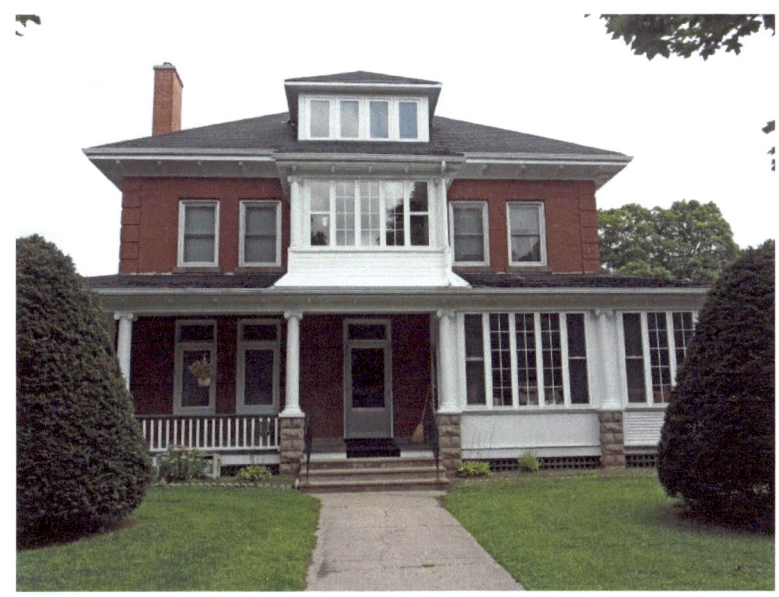

Westport - 11 Church Street - Italianate style - hip roof, dormer, Ionic capitals on verandah pillars

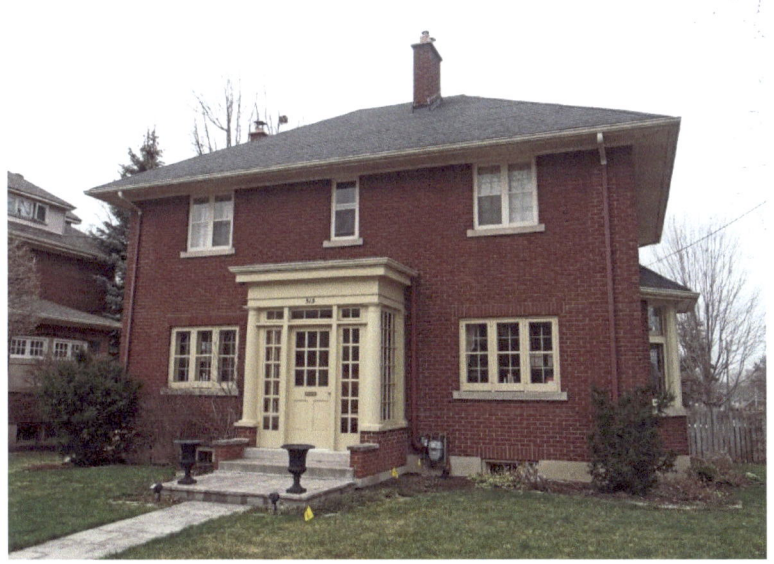

Whitby Book 1 - 513 Centre Street South – Arthur Archibald House – 1928 – hipped roof

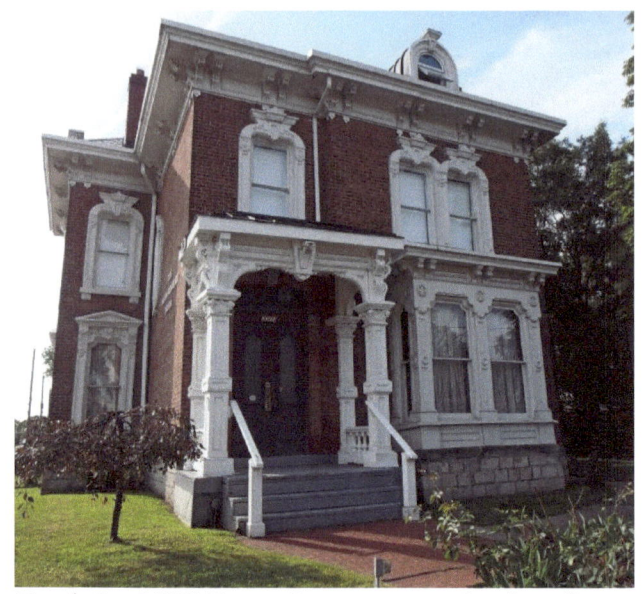

Windsor Book 3 - 3203 Peter Street – cornice brackets, decorative window hoods, ornate porch, dormer

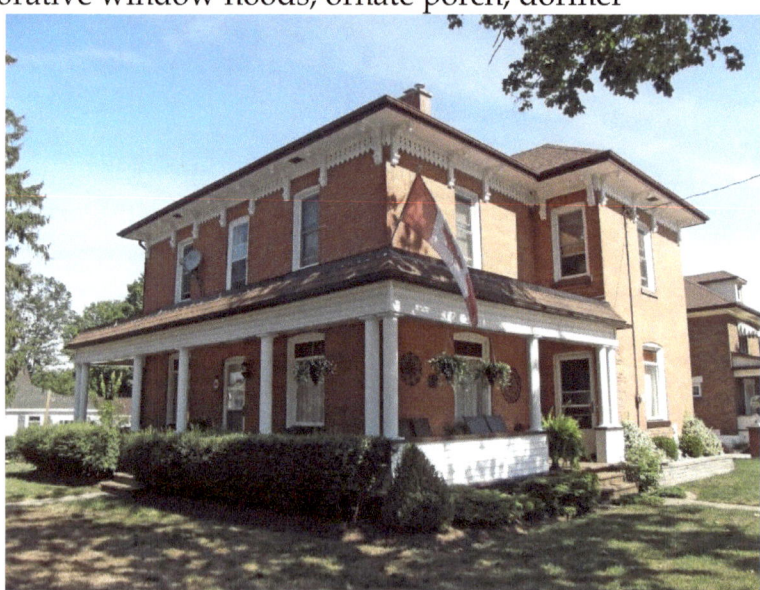

Wingham - #69 - Italianate, cornice brackets, wraparound verandah, decorative cornice

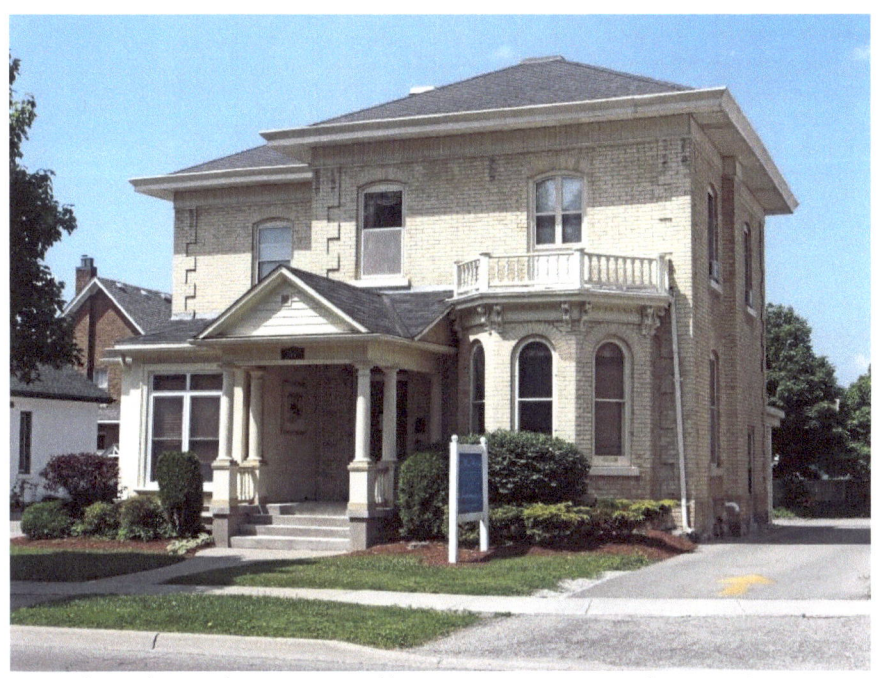

Woodstock Book 2 - 40 Wellington Street South – c. 1874 – Italianate – L shape, two-story, buff brick with decorative quoins, trunked hip roof, large verandah with pediment above steps, Doric columns are supported on wood pedestals and turned balusters

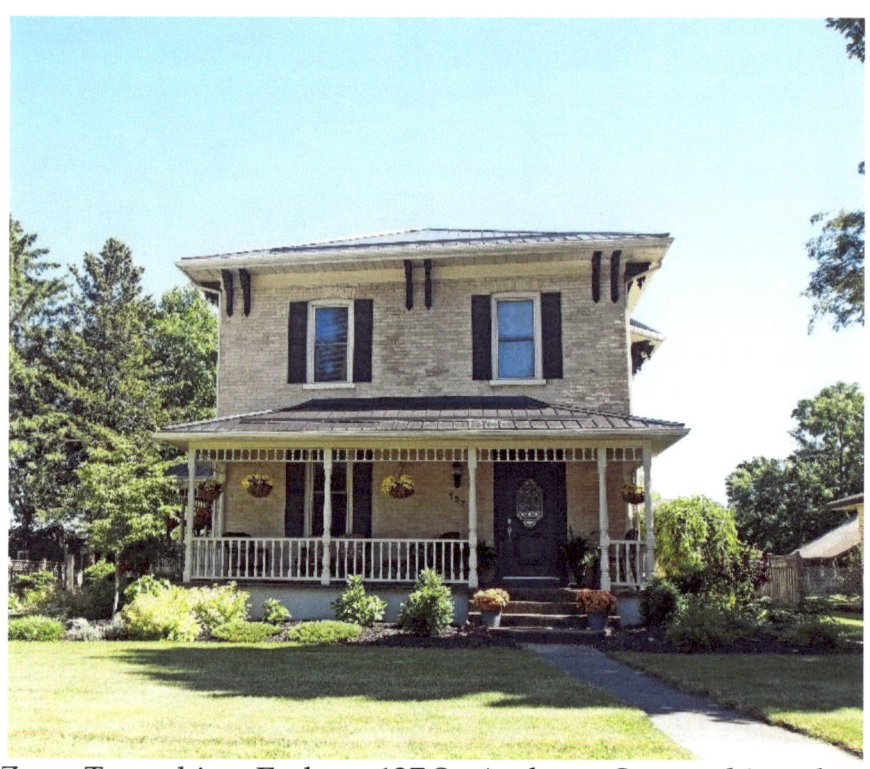

Zorra Township – Embro - 137 St. Andrews Street – hipped roof, cornice brackets

Other Books by Barbara Raue

Coins of Gold
Arrows, Indians and Love
The Life and Times of Barbara
The Cromwell Family Book
Laura Secord Discovered
Daddy Where Are You?

Montana Series
Book 1: Montana Dream
Book 2: Life on the Montana Frontier
Book 3: Montana to Boston and Back
Book 4: Montana Sons Go to War
Book 5: Montana Sons Return from War

Book 1: Rite of Passage
Book 2: Rite of Marriage

© 2020 by Barbara Raue - All the photos in this book have been taken with my cameras. I own the rights to them.

Barbara is The Authority on Saving Our History One Photo at a Time. She is pursuing her interest in photography and architecture by preserving a record through photos of old buildings from the 1800s and 1900s with their unique architecture. Enjoy the beautiful architecture in the comfort of your living room. Dream about what it was like in those by-gone days. Dream about what it was like to live in a mansion like one of those in this book.

Barbara Raue, a wife, mother and grandmother, is an avid reader and writer. She has researched and compiled several family histories. In 2010, Barbara published her book "Coins of Gold," which celebrates the courageous life of her mother, May Todd. Barbara's second book is a historical fiction "Arrows, Indians and Love" which takes place in Boonesborough, Kentucky during the time of Daniel Boone. In 2013, Barbara published *The Cromwell Family Book* in which she traces her ancestry generations back into Great Britain. Her second novel is called *Laura Secord Discovered,* in which the story of Laura's service during the War of 1812 is shared. Barbara's memoir is titled *Daddy Where Are You?* It tells of her life growing up without a father. Five novels in the Montana Series have been published, *Montana Dream, Life on the Montana Frontier, Montana to Boston and Back, Montana Sons Go to War,* and *Montana Sons Return from War. Rite of Passage* and *Rite of Marriage* is a two-book series.

This is a link to Barbara's website to view all of her books
http://barbararaue.ca

www.ingramcontent.com/pod-product-compliance
Lightning Source LLC
Chambersburg PA
CBHW040224220526
45473CB00001B/105